From the library of

The Empty Mirror

Janwillem van de Wetering

The Empty Mirror

Experiences in a Japanese Zen Monastery

Routledge & Kegan Paul   London

First published 1972
by De Driehoek, Amsterdam
as De Lege Spiegal
© *Janwillem van de Wetering 1972*
This translation
first published 1973
by Routledge & Kegan Paul Ltd
Broadway House, 68–74 Carter Lane,
London EC4V 5EL
This translation
© *Janwillem van de Wetering 1973*
Printed in Great Britain by
Alden & Mowbray Ltd
Osney Mead, Oxford
No part of this book may be reproduced in
any form without permission from the
publisher, except for the quotation of brief
passages in criticism

ISBN 0 7100 7578 2

Contents

'The empty mirror.' he said. *'If you could really understand that, there would be nothing left here for you to look for.'*

One

The gate of the monastery, a chicken, and a vendor of noodles

The gate of a monastery in Kyoto, the mystical capital of Japan. Tokyo is the wordly capital, but Kyoto is a holy city, so holy that it was saved by the American bombers in exchange for the Japanese promise that there would be no anti-aircraft guns. Kyoto contains eight thousand temples, mostly Buddhist. I was facing one of these temples, a Zen monastery. I was alone, twenty-six years old, neatly dressed, washed and shaved, for I was applying for a job as a monk, or lay brother. It was a hot morning in the summer of 1958. I had put down my suitcase, which contained only some clothes, books and toilet gear. The taxi which had taken me there had driven off. Around me I saw grey-white plastered walls, about six feet high, topped with tiles made of grey baked clay. Behind the walls were beautifully shaped pine trees, cut and guided by trained and careful hands; behind these rose the temple roof: flat-topped, with sides that sloped down and then turned upwards abruptly at the ends.

I had only been in Japan for a few days. The Dutch ship which brought me from Africa via Bombay, Singapore and Hong Kong had left me in Kobe.

No contact addresses, no acquaintances of acquaintances, no letters of introduction. I did have money, enough for about three years of careful living with a short burst of extravagance now and then. I didn't stay in Kobe, but travelled to Kyoto, an hour's journey by train. I had seen the green Japanese fields, greener even than the green of Holland, mottled with grey advertising boards which, because I couldn't read them, had a surrealistic effect. I had studied my fellow passengers: the men in European, somewhat old-fashioned suits and white shirts, most of them without a tie;

the women in kimonos, small and submissive but with sparkling, curious eyes. Perhaps I seemed curious, too, for they covered their mouths with their hands, looked down and tittered. I understood that although in Europe my size was normal, I was a giant here, a giant and an outsider, a representative of a minority. A student, in a uniform which reminded me of photographs of World War I, addressed me in bad English. Was I a tourist? Yes, a tourist. 'My country is beautiful,' he said. Yes, I could see that. The conversation halted. We smiled at each other, I was given a cigarette which tasted good. I looked out of the window again.

I had been told that Kyoto is a city of temples. Temples and monasteries. Mysterious buildings with puzzling contents. Buildings full of wisdom. And that was what I was looking for. Wisdom, peace, indifference of a high order. Every monastery has a gate, a door, an opening which admits those who look for wisdom, provided the seekers are sincere and honest.

I now looked at the gate in front of me, a wooden structure in the classical Chinese style, with an artfully shaped roof of tiles, and many embellishments; really a small building in itself. The massive doors stood open.

I studied the temple street again. I wasn't alone any more. A chicken walked around my feet, busily looking for food in the sand. In the distance I saw a man approaching, pushing a mobile food-stall, and the wind brought me the smell of fried noodles. He was turning a wooden rattle, and the musical sound would have cheered me up if the thought of the gate hadn't depressed me. In the monastery nobody knew of my arrival. The previous night I had slept in a small hotel. The doorman spoke English, and I had asked him for the address of a Zen monastery, an active monastery, where Zen could be studied. He had looked at me as if my question bewildered him. That type of monastery wasn't open to the public. Why didn't I go to this place or that place— there were gardens there, and statues for anyone to look at. If I liked he would get me a guide; they were proud of their city and he would show me many interesting sights. But I wanted to study Zen.

He didn't understand me. He thought I wanted to spend an

afternoon interviewing a Zen master, that I was a journalist, looking for a story. The idea of my wanting to live in a monastery to become a monk if necessary, to stay for years, seemed beyond him. But I got an address and some directions.

His explanation of how to get there was too intricate for me, so I took a taxi. And now I was where I wanted to be. The noodle-vendor had reached me. He stopped his cart and looked at me invitingly. I nodded. He started filling a bowl with noodles and vegetables. The smell was very good. He hesitated, then offered me a pair of chopsticks; he didn't have a spoon. I didn't know the price and offered him a handful of coins. He hissed politely, breathing in, and selected from my palm a sum equivalent to sixpence. When he saw that I could handle the chopsticks he bowed happily. A noodle which he had dropped to the ground was attacked by the chicken as if it was a living worm, and we both laughed. Well, I thought, the people are not unkind here. Maybe I should give it a try. And I pulled the bell, a huge green-copper bell which hung in the roof of the gate. The noodle-vendor gave a start, bowed hastily, and started pushing his cart away. Later I found out that the bell was holy, only to be used during certain religious ceremonies. Visitors were supposed to enter without announcing themselves. To experience this moment I had made my journey, and broken with the life I had lived up till then. This was the beginning of a new life, a life which I could hardly imagine. A solemn moment. Here I was, new born, a blank page. At once cheerful and nervous, I walked into the temple garden and saw the monastery in its full glory, lower part no longer hidden by the protecting wall. It seemed cool and unchallengeable, sunk in an unassailable peace. It was as if it had grown up from the ground as part of the garden, a garden without flowers, laid out with rocks, shrubs, trees and neatly raked paths. And moss everywhere—many varieties of moss, from soft grey to deepest green. Quiet, peaceful colours. The monk who came towards me didn't seem at all peaceful. I had difficulty in recognizing this apparition as a man of the present time. A ludicrous dwarf, on wooden sandals supported by laths, so that he walked about two inches off the ground. With his wide black gown, drawn up in a white belt so that his legs showed to just below the knees, he might, at first sight, have been taken for a woman, a washerwoman or a charwoman, interrupted while busy with buckets and mops. He approached quickly and the wide sleeves of his gown flapped nervously about him. His head had been shaved and his smile, the refuge of every agitated Japanese, seemed tinny because his teeth were made of silver.

A few paces from me he stopped and bowed. This bow was quite different from what I had got used to. The Japanese always bow when greeting you, but usually quickly and from habit, without much care—the back is bent and then returns to its normal position. But this bow was solemn and almost military. He kept his hands on his thighs and bowed stiffly from his waist, so that his hands glided down far below his knees. I imitated the bow as well as I could.

'Good day,' the monk said in English. 'What do you want?'

'I want to meet your master,' I said. 'I want to ask him if I can be allowed to live here.'

Although I spoke slowly and clearly, he appeared not to understand me. I pointed to my suitcase, and then at the temple. He followed my explaining index-finger and looked at my face, but comprehension had not yet dawned. We looked at each other for a few seconds in silence, and then he gestured to me to follow him.

In the temple porch he pointed to my shoes, and I took them off. Then he pointed at a statue of Buddha, visible between the open temple doors made of lattice-work and paper. I bowed in front of the Buddha just as the monk had bowed to me. Then we climbed the wooden stairs together and I was taken to a room where he left me alone. To reach this room he had to open two doors, sliding doors moving between wooden rails. Each time he knelt on the thick straw mats which form the floor of Japanese rooms, opened the door respectfully, waited till I had entered, and then repeated the ceremony at the other side of the door to close it. I was on holy ground. There were no chairs in the temple room and I sat down uncomfortably on the floor. I should have liked to light a cigarette but there was no ashtray and I thought that it would be impolite to smoke in such surroundings without having been invited to. Behind me was a niche, built from unpainted and unplaned wood which could have been smooth, thin tree-trunks or thick branches; it contained another statue, this time a lifesize image of a Japanese or Chinese monk, in the meditation position of the double lotus.* His glass eyes stared, unfocusing, towards the floor, gazing at a point about nine feet away. Nobody came in and I had time to observe the statue at my leisure. There was a striking difference between the Buddha statue in the temple porch and this monk. The Buddha appeared loving because of its faint smile; it exhaled peace, mixed with compassion. This monk seemed different, powered by will, more intense. The lips were drawn in to an expression of tremendous concentration, aimed at a subject which couldn't be of this earth. A superhuman force came from this statue, an intense energy. But the two statues also looked alike in a way, for both were free, free of any care which can be felt or imagined. Later I was told that this statue represented the founder of the monastery, a Zen master who lived in the Middle Ages, one of the most spectacular characters from the history of Zen.

The wooden master intrigued me, but when his glass eyes began to frighten me, I turned and looked outside. It was a warm day and the garden doors were open. Behind me smouldered incense, and the heavy smell calmed my mind. The doors gave on to a veranda behind which I could see a rockgarden with a pond where red goldfish swam about in a leisurely way, nibbling at pieces of bread which had been thrown into the water. Suddenly a monk came past, mopping the veranda. He was pressing on a large rag with flat palms, while moving his legs quickly. He made me think of a scene in old-fashioned comedy film. A little later he came back, moving in the same fashion, and this time he looked like a large bug or waterbeetle. Although I was gazing at the garden I still saw the wooden statue of the master and I felt

---

* In this position the legs are crossed in such a way that the left foot is turned round to rest on the right thigh and the right foot on the left thigh. The back is held straight and the hands are folded, resting in the bowl formed by the feet.

threatened by the will-power of the man. I couldn't know then that he was the legendary master who, having become a master after many years' training, didn't use his title, but made himself unfindable for twenty years. He lived with the dregs of society under the bridges of Kyoto and didn't show any outward sign of being different from them. The emperor, a follower of Zen, heard that a great master was hidden in his city. A rumour went round that the master kept company with the scum of the city. The emperor was told that the master fancied a certain type of melon. The emperor disguised himself, took a basket full of melons and walked through the city till, under a bridge, he found a beggar with remarkable sparkling eyes. He offered the beggar a melon and said: 'Take the melon without using your hands.' The beggar answered: 'Give me the melon without using your hands.' The emperor then donated money to build a temple and installed the master as a teacher.

I remembered, sitting in the temple room and waiting for someone to show himself, that I had heard that looking for God is a two-fold movement. The seeker tries to find a way by climbing painfully, but he is, without at first being aware of it, pulled up as well. It would be nice, I thought, if this strong master would make a little effort and guide me towards the higher regions.

While I was thinking the monk came in. I made a confused bow, and the monk nodded and gestured in an inviting manner.

We returned to the porch, where I put on my shoes again. After a short walk through a pathway, roofed in the same way as the gate, we arrived at a small house. I understood that this must be the house of the monastery teacher. I had read that Zen masters live apart and do not worry about the running of the monastery. The daily routine passes them by; their task is the spiritual direction of the monks and other disciples whom they receive every day, one by one.

We came to another porch and I saw a pair of large-sized western-style shoes standing between the Japanese sandals. The monk pushed the door aside and disappeared. I was in a room with an old Japanese gentleman and a young wide-shouldered westerner who looked at me attentively. I bowed, in the prescribed manner, and was acknowledged by two friendly nods.

'Sit down' the westerner said in American-sounding English. I estimated him to be in his early thirties and it struck me that his jeans and striped summer shirt didn't clash with the surroundings. 'My name is Peter,' the American said, 'and you are lucky that I was in the neighbourhood, because the only language here is Japanese. The master would like to know why you want to put your suitcase in the temple hall.' After that the conversation was between the master and myself. The American translated and didn't comment on anything that was said.

I had read enough about Zen masters to know that they do not like long stories and prefer methods without words. According to the books Zen masters will shout suddenly, trip you up while out for a quiet walk, beat you on the head or say something which, apparently, doesn't make sense at all. It seemed to me that it would be better to make my statements as short and concise as possible.

'I am here,' I said carefully, 'to get to know the purpose of life. Buddhism knows that purpose, the purpose which I am trying to find, and Buddhism knows the way which leads to enlightenment.' While I tried to explain my intentions in this way I already felt ridiculous. I felt that life *must* have a purpose, and it seemed very stupid to have to admit that I didn't know the purpose of the creation of what is around us and also what is within us. But I didn't know what else to say. To my surprise the master answered immediately. I had thought that he would be silent. When the Buddha was asked if life has, or does not have, a purpose, if there is, or isn't, a life after death, if the universe has, or does not have, an end, if we can speak of a first cause or not, he did not answer, but maintained a 'noble silence'. He would have done that to indicate that these questions about life were not expressed in the right way. Our brains are given to us as instruments, capable of a specific, a limited task. When trying to understand the real mysteries, the brain stops short. The brain can contain neither the questions themselves, nor the answers. To come to real understanding, to enlightenment, quite another instrument has to be used.

Intuitive insight has to be developed by following the eightfold path, the Buddhist method. What Buddha wanted was that his disciples should use the method which he had found and perfected. Buddha was a practical, a pragmatic man.

But the Zen master, in his simple grey gown, an old man, well into his seventies, but with clear glittering eyes, did not maintain a noble silence.

'That's fine,' he said. 'Life has a purpose, but a strange purpose. When you come to the end of the road and find perfect insight you will see that enlightenment is a joke.' 'A joke,' said the American, and stared seriously at me. 'Life is a joke; you'll learn to understand that sometime—not now, but it will come.'

I asked if I could be accepted as a disciple. The teacher nodded. His consent surprised me. Obviously the books which I had read about Zen were faulty, written by inexperienced writers. Zen masters, I had been assured, do not readily accept disciples. Admission is always apparently blocked by obstacles. The disciple is told that the master is too old, or too ill, or too busy, to accept new disciples. Or the disciple hears that he hasn't developed himself sufficiently to become a disciple but that he can be admitted, temporarily, as a woodcutter or farm labourer.

But no, I could be accepted. If (there was a condition) I was prepared to stay for eight months; during a shorter period I wouldn't be able to learn anything. 'I can stay three years,' I said. 'That isn't necessary,' said the master. 'Three years is a long time in a man's life. You do not have to commit yourself, or promise anything, but you should stay eight months. That period you'll have to fix in your mind—you should get used to the thought that you have to be here for eight months. It isn't easy here. We get up at three o'clock in the morning and we do not go to bed before eleven at night. We meditate a lot, there is work in the garden, there's a lot of tension, and you'll have the extra problem of being in a very strange environment. Everything will be different for you, the language, the way we sit, the food. You can't make use of anything you have learned. But that is good; a little extra training will be all right.'

The master spoke for a long time, interrupting himself every

8

now and then so that Peter could catch up with the translation. When he finished I thought this to be a good opportunity to ask a few questions. I tried to formulate intelligent questions but they all boiled down to the same thing: does life have a purpose or not? The master shook his head. 'I could answer your questions but I won't try because you wouldn't understand the answer. Now listen. Imagine that I am holding a pot of tea, and you are thirsty. You want me to give you tea. I can pour tea but you'll have to produce a cup. I can't pour the tea on your hands or you'll get burnt. If I pour it on the floor I shall spoil the floormats. You have to have a cup. That cup you will form in yourself by the training you will receive here.'

The idea of drinking tea had made him thirsty and he said a few words to Peter, who bowed respectfully and went outside. He was back at once carrying a tray, with a pot of tea, cups, a dish full of sugarcakes, cigarettes and an ashtray.

The master relaxed, and the atmosphere in the room changed. Peter leant against the wall and the master rubbed his back against one of the poles of the niche in the wall. I shifted my position as well; I had been kneeling and my legs hurt.

'You come from Holland,' the master said. 'I have read about your country. You got the land from the water by building dikes and by pumping the water out. Sometimes the water streams back again and you build new dikes and start all over again.'

'There has been a war between our countries,' I said, 'between your country and mine.'

'Yes,' the master said, 'there has been a great war. Many of my disciples died in the war. War is an exercise. Now we have peace and people exercise themselves in a different manner. Much is built, only to be destroyed suddenly and then built again. Do you hold it against us, us Japanese, this war?'

'No,' I said. 'I lived in Holland during the war. I associate evil, the despicable, cruelty, with German uniforms, with German soldiers. Japan, for me, has no associations. I have seen a little piece of your country and I thought it beautiful, and the faces of the people were kind.'

The master smiled. I was given another sugarcake and another cup of green bitter tea. After that the interview came to an end. The master straightened his back, Peter came back to the kneeling position and I got up and bowed.

The monk had been waiting for me outside. He had my suitcase. 'Your room,' he said, and pointed to a small building at the other side of the garden. The building proved to be neglected: the room I was given was large, but very dirty. The floormats were badly worn and the paper and latticework which formed the front wall was torn and broken.

The monk brought a broom, some rags and a bucket. He showed me a tap in the courtyard behind the building. Then he produced a roll of paper and some tools and started repairing the front wall. It took a few hours, but by then the room was reasonably clean and when we had finished and he had also fixed the windows and door he smiled, bowed, and returned to the main temple. I lay down on the floor and supported my head on my suitcase. A small dish I had found served as an ashtray. I smoked contentedly. Here I am, I thought, arrived at the source of wisdom. I have a good chance of getting to know something. Still, I didn't feel quite safe. This was a very strange environment. An eastern temple with a sloping roof, walls of paper, low beams to knock your head against, small living shapes in black cotton gowns. The last thought which flitted through my mind before I fell asleep was that it might have been a better idea to have bought an old converted fishing boat to sail on the Dutch inland sea.

Two

Meditating hurts

Clack. A dry sound. Somebody knocking two pieces of wood together, I thought. I pulled a thin piece of string, switching on a weak light bulb. Three o'clock at night. Why would anyone, at three o'clock at night, knock two pieces of wood together? Ah yes, I thought, I am in a monastery. I have promised to get up at three o'clock at night, for eight months. Confused and angry thoughts jostled each other in my head while I quickly dressed, knocking my head against a beam. It was cold, and my eyelids were stuck together with sleep. I knocked my head again and found myself outside, shivering and listening to new sounds. The monk who had woken me was now waking others a few hundred yards away. I heard him knocking his clappers together and shouting the names of his colleagues whom he wanted to rouse. In the temple a bell was rung, and somewhere else a gong boomed. I washed my face and hands in the courtyard and combed my hair. I couldn't see what I was doing; there was no light, no mirror, and no time to shave. I knew that I had three minutes, from the moment of waking, to get to the meditation hall. The evening before, Peter had explained the daily routine a little. Everything had to happen quickly—there was no time for hesitation, no time to turn around and have another little snooze. Get up, dress, wash, and go to the meditation hall.

The large hall was situated at the other side of the garden. It consisted of an empty space with high wide forms on both sides. On the forms were straw mats and cushions, one stack of cushions for each monk. In the centre of the hall stood a large altar with a statue of Manjusri, the Bodhisatva of meditation, holding a sword to cut thoughts. Smouldering incense. When you enter you have to bow to Manjusri and then bow again to the head monk who sits near the entrance, positioned in such a way that he can control the entire hall. Then you walk to your cushions and you bow again. The cushions are holy because on those cushions you are supposed to find, sometime, enlightenment, freedom, the end of all your problems.

Then you sit down quickly, twisting your legs together and stretching your back. You stare straight ahead of you, wide-eyed, and the meditation begins as the head monk hits his bell. Twenty-five minutes later he hits his bell again. When everything goes as it should go you will by then have been absolutely silent for twenty-five minutes, breathing quietly and deep in concentration.

You may now slip outside but you have to be back within five minutes. Then the next period of twenty-five minutes starts. After two periods the monks, one by one, leave to visit the master in his little house, and then there is breakfast, boiling hot rice gruel and pickled vegetables, washed down with Chinese tea without sugar. Peter, when he explained it all to me, had made me sit down on the cushions while we were in the meditation hall. 'Put your right foot on your left thigh,' he said. I couldn't do it. 'Try and cross your legs then.' I could manage that, and got myself into a position resembling the way a tailor sits. 'Try it again.' Peter said, but it proved quite impossible; my thigh muscles were too short and too stiff. He nodded his head sadly. 'It'll hurt,' he predicted, 'but you'll have to learn.'

'Can't I meditate on a chair?'

'Why?' he asked scornfully. 'Are you an old man? Or an invalid? Nonsense. You are young, you can bend your body, and those muscles will stretch in time. When you fold your legs your thighs will drop under their own weight and gradually your muscles will lengthen. If you exercise a little every day you'll be able to sit in the half lotus within a few months, and in the full lotus within a few years. I once had the same trouble as you have now. And I was, if that's possible, even more stiff than you are'.

'But what's so important about this lotus business?'

'To be able to concentrate well your spirit has to be in balance;

when your spirit is in balance your body has to be in balance as well. The double lotus is a position of pure balance, of real balance. When you sit in the full lotus, you just have to become quiet because nothing else can happen. Your heart quietens down, your breathing becomes calm, your thoughts stop flitting about. When you hold your back and head straight all the nerve centres in your body start working in the right way. If you don't like the double lotus, if you don't even want to try to master it, you cause yourself needless trouble; and yet you cling to the illusion that you are making things easy and pleasant.'

'But isn't it possible to meditate on a chair?'

'You can meditate in any attitude,' replied Peter, 'but one is best, and that's the one we'll teach you. You will be here for eight months and we'll teach you all sorts of things. Now be obedient, and don't talk all the time. The more you talk, the more you defend yourself, the more time you waste. Perhaps you have a lot of time to waste but we are very busy people.'

'Zen is free,' I thought. 'Free of worry, loose, detached. Free and easy. Bah.'

Who Peter was I found out later. He had arrived in Japan as an American soldier, part of the army which came to occupy the empire. There he had met the Zen master, by accident, in the street. The meeting had made such an impression on him that he had later returned to Japan. Like me, he had once walked through the monastery gate, but with a difference, for he knew the master. He had lived in the monastery for a year or so, and now had his own house in the neighbourhood. He earned his living as a concert pianist and he taught singing, but every morning or every night (three o'clock in the morning was always the middle of the night to me) he came to see the master, and most evenings he came to the monastery to meditate. When I met him he had been a disciple of the master for more than ten years. An advanced soul.

I thought, at first, that the monastery would place me under him, that I would be connected to him in some way, but during the first year I hardly saw him. When he arrived he went straight to the hall and when the meditation was over he went straight home. He spent a lot of time with the master, but I wasn't admitted to the master's house. The master only received me in the morning after the early meditation, and these visits were formal, the master seated on a small platform, the disciple kneeling respectfully. There was no intimate contact. Japan is a formal country with strict rules of behaviour. I sometimes met the teacher accidentally in the garden and if I wanted to ask him something at such an occasion it could be done, but I couldn't just walk into his room like Peter, or the head monk.

As I was going to deal only with the Japanese I had to learn the Japanese language, An old lady in the neighbourhood was prepared to give me daily lessons, so every afternoon I spent an hour with her, and in my room I spent an hour or two a day on homework. Slowly I began to understand the language a little but it took a long time, half a year at least, before I started to stammer more or less fluently. I never learned to speak Japanese correctly.

The first meditation is forever etched into my memory. After a few minutes the first pains started. My thighs began to tremble like violin strings. The sides of my feet became burning pieces of wood. My back, kept straight with difficulty, seemed to creak and to shake involuntarily. Time passed inconceivably slowly. There was no concentration at all. I hadn't been given anything to concentrate on anyway, so I just sat and waited for the bell to ring, the bell which would finish the period of agony.

Later I was able to study other beginners, westerners and Japanese. I never saw anyone who was as stiff as I was when I started. Mostly they could find some way of sitting in balance but I had to spend three months on top of an anthill before I stopped wobbling, and could get one foot up. The worst was over then, although I didn't stop suffering at once. There are many kinds of suffering.

I believe that meditation is difficult for everybody. Our personality forces us to be active, we walk up and down, we gesticulate, we tell stories, we crack jokes, to prove to ourselves and to others that we exist, that our individuality is important.

We are frightened of silence, of our own thoughts. We want

to play some music or see a film. We like to be distracted. We want to put things together, light cigarettes, have a drink, look out of the window. All these occupations fall away during meditation.

In Zen there is an exercise called *kinhin*. The monks, after sitting still for some hours, walk in a circle while they continue their concentration. Only the head monk, who is in charge of the exercise, watches the time and looks where he is going; the others follow.

When I took part in a *kinhin* exercise for the first time I had to break away from the circle and slip out of the hall. I leant against a tree and laughed till the tears were running down my face. I, a wanderer, a beatnik (there were no hippies then), a free soul, now formed part of a queue and kept time.

Meditation is an exercise aimed at detachment, at loosening one's ties. I was bound by the idea, which I had created myself, that I was not bound to anything. A Japanese physician who often joined the monks during the evening's meditation, told me that he always had trouble stopping himself from tittering when he sat there quietly and tried to concentrate. To sit still is a way of creating distance, of isolating oneself, of breaking away not only from what happens around us but also from what happens within, in the mind itself. Later, when I was given a *koan* to concentrate on, I noticed how the most trivial matters can break concentration. A memory of a good soup, eaten years ago in some restaurant or other, provided enough subject matter to spend ten minutes on the most disconnected facts and associations. To meditate is to sit still, in the right attitude, and to concentrate on never mind what subject. Buddha, Christ, a pebble, nothing, a vacuum, the thin blue sky, God, love, it doesn't matter. In Zen training concentration is on the *koan*, a subject which the master presents to the disciple. One tries to become one with the *koan*, to close the distance between oneself and the *koan*, to lose oneself in the *koan*, till everything drops or breaks away and nothing is left but the *koan* which fills the universe. And if that point is reached enlightenment, the revelation, follows. Very simple, but quite impossible, or apparently impossible; for if it were *not* possible, all mystical training would be in vain. But mysticism is as old as the world, and 'free souls', 'wise men', 'holy men', 'prophets', 'adepts', 'arhats', 'bodhisatva's, 'buddha's' have come out of all schools and all exercises. In every training the ego is broken, the 'I' is crushed.

It is almost impossible, especially for the beginner, to meditate alone. In a group, where it is arranged beforehand how long the meditation will last, it is possible. Our pride, or our shame, will force us not to stop the exercise before the arranged time. If others can do it, I can do it. Pride isn't always negative—as a means to an end it can be used profitably. The others don't wobble, and that's why I won't wobble. I am too proud to groan with pain. I am too proud to scratch my neck. I am sitting still, just like the others. If everyone thinks that way the group sits still. That is not to say that I didn't do a lot of wobbling and groaning, for pride has its limits. The pain was sometimes so bad that I imagined that I was sitting on a pile of burning, crackling wood, and my teeth would chatter and I would sob, unable to restrain myself at all. If it got that bad the head monk would notice and send me outside for a period of twenty-five minutes. I would then have to walk up and down while continuing my concentration, always in a part of the garden where he could see me from his seat near the door of the meditation hall.

The first day in the monastery passed quietly. After the early morning meditation I wasn't admitted to the master's room, but sent to my own room. Someone came to fetch me for breakfast. We sat on the floor at low tables, in the lotus position of course, although I was allowed to kneel. This was easier but also painful after a while, for the dining room had a hard wooden floor. Before eating the monks sang a *sutra*, one of the Buddha's sermons, in classical Chinese, while the cook hit a wooden drum to keep time. It was a hypnotic sound, that singing, short and staccato, the monks cutting the words into syllables and droning them with sharp, abrupt endings. After that we were given small bowls filled with rice and hot water and another bowl containing pickled vegetables; these didn't taste too bad. We were also served *takuan*, an orange radish, pickled and sliced. I put a few slices in my mouth but they were very sharp and I grimaced, sucking my cheeks in and looking about desperately, as I felt sweat prickle under my hair. One wasn't supposed to speak at table but everyone giggled, even the severe head monk when they saw my reaction to the delicacy. Later, when I got used to the taste, I even began to like *takuan* and used to help myself secretly when I passed through the kitchen.

After breakfast we worked. I was given a mop and taken to a very long corridor. There were other corridors to be cleaned when I had finished the first. Eventually someone rang a bell and we had an hour off. I went to my room and fell asleep; it was 6 a.m., still very early.

At seven, I followed the others to the vegetable garden to harvest cucumbers. The monks wore overalls, and they laughed and talked, pushing and tackling each other. Most of them were young, between seventeen and twenty-one. A few were older, but I only got to know the young ones; the older monks kept to themselves.

The head monk had his own room. Because he was the practical leader of the monastery and because he was a priest, and therefore higher in rank than the others, he was treated with respect. He received guests, took care of the administration of the monastery, paid the bills, collected gifts, wrote letters. My monthly payment was arranged with him—about £2 a month for board and lodging, the lowest rate I ever paid in my life.

Another older monk worked as cook. The daily menu was simple: vegetables, rice, barley gruel, no meat at all, sometimes fried noodles or a dish which resembles the Chinese *tjap tjoy*, a vegetable stew which the cook could make very tasty. We also had feasts from time to time and then the cook had three or four assistants and prepared complicated dishes. But mostly the fare was very simple and not very nourishing, a diet which didn't do much for me. Within a few weeks I began to feel ill and weak. The monks called a doctor and he prescribed better food, so I was given permission to get a meal from outside once a day (if it was possible to go out, for sometimes the monastery cut itself off from the outside world and closed its gates for a week) and I found a small restaurant close by where I could get fried rice and meat salads.

In the afternoon the meditation started again: four periods, two hours in all. Dinner was early, at 4 p.m., and was the last meal of the day. In the evening we meditated from seven till ten. Meditation times differ in a Zen monastery. In winter there is more sitting than in summer, but I found even this light summer training of six hours a day far more than I could really put up with. Even so, I got through it. I had to of course—my pride wouldn't let me back out of it.

I have read warnings that meditation can be dangerous and should only be done under the personal supervision of a master. I don't believe this is true. If a group of reasonably sane people want to sit together for an hour or so, it will work perfectly well. However, if certain members of the group want to see mystical light and astral helpers and visions and lofty spirits bathing in a sea of high-powered radiance, a nervous atmosphere may be caused which can have unpleasant temporary results. Buddhism is for the average, normal man. It is a method of transforming daily life, the comings and goings and activities of a common man, into a mystical training. Buddhism is no school for magicians. You can't predict the future with it, and you can't use it to find out if you were Louis XIV in a previous life. Nor is it advisable to use Buddhism as a means of developing the third eye, to see the colours of the auras of our fellow men.

In China a Zen master travelled with a few disciples to the capital and camped near the river. A monk of another sect asked one of the disciples of the Zen master if his teacher could do magic tricks. His own master, said the monk of the other sect, was a very talented and developed man. If he stood on this side of the river, and somebody else stood on the other side, and if you gave the master a brush and the other a sheet of paper then the master would be able to write characters in the air which would appear on the sheet of paper. The Zen monk replied that his master was also a very talented and developed man, because he too could perform the most astounding feats. If he slept, for instance, he slept, and if he ate, he ate.

In Tibet in particular, schools were developed which originated from a mixture of Buddhism and other methods. The followers of these schools claimed that they had all sorts of supernatural powers: they could fly, they could manifest themselves in different places at the same time, they could make objects disappear and appear again at another spot. It is quite possible that these claims are true, but I wonder if this type of supernatural happening has any real value. Zen masters have often given their opinion of this sort of thing. Supernatural gifts are obstacles on the way to enlightenment, insight, true understanding. The Buddha himself never boasted about his supernatural power. He taught the method of the eightfold path and set an example to show the way.

While I was in the monastery I was continually referred back to the daily routine, the simple everyday life. If I wanted to expound some clever theory I was either ignored or ridiculed or curtly told not to talk nonsense. What mattered was 'here and now', whatever I happened to be doing, whether I was peeling potatoes in the kitchen, washing rice, pulling out weeds, learning Japanese, drinking tea, or meditating. I had to solve my *koan*, the subject of my meditation, and I shouldn't fuss.

It is irritating, annoying, to be shut up all the time, to be unable to talk, not to be able to say: 'Here I am, I have experienced something, I have thought of something, I believe I know something, I understand something, please listen to me.' What irritated me most, I think, was that nobody wanted to listen to me when I discovered that meditation, even the blundering sort of meditation I was engaged in, led to new experiences with colour and shape. I noticed that when I walked through the temple garden, the observation of bits of moss on rocks, or a slowly moving goldfish, or reeds swaying with the wind, led to ecstasy.

By losing myself in the colours and shapes around me I seemed to become very detached, an experience which I had known before, in Africa, after using hashish. The feeling wasn't only caused by observing, being aware of, 'beautiful' things, such as goldfish or pieces of moss; a full dustbin or dogshit with flies around it led to exactly the same result. And this 'getting high' was much more satisfactory than the hashish experiences, because now I felt happy and quiet and sometimes pleasantly tense, whereas I had never known quite where I was with hashish—sometimes the experience was pleasant, but often it was nasty and full of fear. Hashish had also given me negative and confusing visions, such as the sudden appearance of endless highways in a strange, unreal light, while now I wasn't bothered by visions at all. I merely seemed to really see what I was looking at. I tried to find an explanation and concluded that we are, under normal everyday stress and circumstances, much too tense and rushed to be able to be fully aware. None of the senses will then function properly; and we do and think too much at the same time, with the result that nothing succeeds. Alcohol, or hashish, or engaging in some intense and dangerous activity like riding a motorcycle, gives us the only chance to channel our attention in a single direction. A tree is a fantastic example of beauty, but who has time to look at a tree?

And now that suddenly, unexpectedly, without even wanting to, I could suddenly observe and really see objects in my surroundings, I thought this event of such importance that I wanted my discovery to be acknowledged, accepted by qualified authorities. But the master didn't show the slightest interest; he wouldn't even give me one of his rare nods. He thought it quite normal that moss on rocks and full dustbins are visually interesting—a truth so obvious that any comment is wasted. Zen monasteries are severe and tough.

Even so, I was occasionally praised, even specially invited by the head monk to his private room and treated to bitter tea and sweet cakes, without having any idea of what it was that I had done right. At one time I was tea 'monk' in the meditation hall for a few weeks (I never wore monk's clothes in the monastery always jeans and a black jersey, and in winter a black duffel coat). After the third meditation period I had to slip out quietly, rush to the kitchen, make tea in a large kettle, and then get back as quickly as possible. In the hall my return was greeted by the head monk striking his bell and I had to bow to the altar. Then I gave everyone tea, I didn't have to bother about the cups as another monk provided them beforehand. But on one occasion I found this hadn't happened. I stood there with the kettle and nobody had a cup. I looked surprised, understood that I couldn't just stand about, put the kettle down, bowed to the altar and went back to the kitchen to fetch cups. Everything which is done in a Zen temple is part of a scheme, even the most trivial activities are part of a ceremonial tradition, but there is no tradition for cups which aren't there. So I created a new ceremony on the spot, came back with a tray full of cups which I had found in a cupboard (they weren't the right cups but I hadn't had the time to look for them properly), bowed with tray and all to the altar and the Bodhisatva, gave everyone a cup, put the tray against the back of the altar, and poured tea. It seemed an acceptable way of dealing with an unexpected situation. My teachers, the master himself, the head monk, and later Peter, thought this a matter of importance. I had proved, so I was told three times, that I was a good pupil. Zen training fosters awareness: it produces somebody who concentrates on everything he does, who tries to do everything as well as possible and who becomes aware of his circumstances and of the part which he plays within his environment. If an unexpected situation suddenly develops he will know how to handle it, and will, by saving himself, save others. The monk who had forgotten the cups wasn't scolded—everyone had had his tea.

Zen masters are actors. The feather which had been stuck in my cap three times, by the head monk who called me to his room, by the master who spoke to me in the garden, and by Peter who patted me on the shoulder when he met me in the kitchen, was in itself of no significance. Teacups or no teacups, the case in itself wasn't worth mentioning. I had felt flattered at first, but when they really overdid it I understood that they were really trying to tell me something about awareness.

Meanwhile the meditation continued, day after day. Sometimes six hours a day, sometimes eight, sometimes twelve. The first week of the month the monastery closed its gates, the monks received no mail and the telephone was cut. The master saw us not once, but three times a day. After a month I was admitted to the master's room for the first time. First I had to practise the ceremony of 'seeing the master' while he wasn't there. The head monk took the part of master. He sat on the platform and stared at me with a nasty glint in his eye. I had to come in slowly, with my hands folded, bow, prostrate myself three times on the floor, and then kneel. After the interview was over I would have to do the same in reverse, and leave the room walking backwards. I had to try a few times before the head monk was satisfied and he told me to learn to walk more softly, because my greater length and weight caused the floormats to start bouncing a little and the movement might bother the master.

Although I was beginning to feel fanatical about Zen, I thought this approach was overdone, just as saluting and coming to attention in the army had seemed ridiculous and senseless to me. I shooed the rebellious thought away by producing the idea that the Zen master himself had to be a free, completely detached man and these were no more than good manners, of no real importance and merely created for appearances of order and respect.

The head monk had advised me not to read while I was in the monastery. I didn't pay much attention to this and read a biography of Milarepa, the most famous Tibetan Buddhist holy man.* Milarepa hadn't had an easy start either. When he found his teacher Marpa, Milarepa was a black magician who had repented and seen the errors of his ways. Marpa made Milarepa do exercises to counteract the results of his own evil deeds. He had to build houses, and every time he finished a house Marpa said that he had made a mistake about the site. The house shouldn't be here, but there, on that hilltop. And then Milarepa had to take his house to pieces again and carry the stones, one by one, to the hilltop where he would build the house again only to be told to pull it down once more. It didn't seem such a terrible punishment to me. I should have preferred to build houses, even while knowing that I would have to take them down again, rather than meditate in a hall where I was being slowly torn to pieces.

* *The Life of Milarepa*, by his pupil Lobzang Jivaka, translated into English by W. Y. Evans-Wentz, John Murray, (1962).

Further on in the book I found descriptions of Milarepa's meditation, but nowhere did it mention that he had any trouble. There was nothing about pain in the legs or back, the fight with sleep, the confused and endlessly interrupting thoughts.

Sleep had never been a source of trouble for me, but now it had become a fierce opponent. I slept for four hours a night and another hour during the day, provided nobody interfered by ringing a bell or beating a gong indicating that something had to be done somewhere. I had learned the meaning of the various signals. Every day *sutras* were sung in the temple room and I would have to be there with the others. I couldn't join in, the chanting was too foreign to me and I couldn't read the characters of the text, so I had to content myself with kneeling down and listening to the monks; sometimes I literally fell over with sleep. Because I couldn't master the lotus position I couldn't achieve balance, while the monks, who were very comfortable in the lotus, could afford to fall asleep while meditating as they didn't risk falling over and making a spectacle of themselves. There were days which seemed so hopeless that I had to use all my strength to get up in the morning. When I tried to visualise the immediate future I saw nothing but pictures of bondage and assorted difficulties. Sometimes I didn't get up and pretended to have a sore throat or a headache but I couldn't do that too often. I hadn't come to the monastery to try and escape from the monastic training.

I missed the company of my friends. The monks made jokes but they were different from the jokes my friends would invent. I wished for the company of just one of my former mates, so that we could laugh together about the many seemingly illogical or contrasting situations. I missed my motorcycle and it annoyed me that I couldn't listen to jazz, although the music of the temple, the chanting voices of the monks, the clappers, cymbals, wooden drums and gongs fascinated me. I would have liked to have some coffee now and then and not just Chinese tea. And most of all I wanted to sit on a western-style lavatory, with a cup of coffee, a cigar, and a book, and not, as now, have to squat down uncomfortably above a hole in a board with flies coming out of it.

Three

Life is suffering

The ship which took me to Japan carried very few passengers. There was sufficient second-class accommodation for a hundred people but there were only three of us, and my two fellow passengers turned out to be moody Danish soldiers who spoke nothing but Danish. They were travelling to the Far East at their own expense to catch up with their ship, which they had missed in Durban because they got drunk. They hardly talked to each other, and spent most of their time hanging dejectedly over the railing. Sometimes they drank beer and sang sad songs with a lot of 'ø's and 'flø's.

I didn't mind having to spend five weeks at sea. It meant another five weeks's holiday in the shadow of the monastery, and I had time to read. I thought that a little theoretical knowledge in the Buddhist field might come in useful, and I read dutifully and made schemes on large sheets of paper, with neat arrows and connecting lines. In this way I learned something about the teaching of Buddha. The first truth of Buddhism is that life means suffering. Life = suffering.

According to the myth Buddha was guided to awareness of the first truth by highly placed heavenly personages who wanted him to show the way to a better pattern of life. Buddha had once been a spoiled prince who lived in a luxurious palace. At his birth a peculiar and mysterious light had been observed in the sky and some courtiers said that they heard heavenly music. His father, ruler over a small kingdom, called in astrologists who predicted that the child had an exceptional personality and would become either a

world ruler or an enlightened spirit who would solve the
questions of the universe and who would be able to
show the way to the mysteries to others as well. The
father decided to take his son along a purely worldly path.
The son should be given the impression that material things,
wealth, success, power, are ideals which have a permanent
as well as an essential value. Old people, sick people, poor
people, depressed people, anyone miserable in any way,
were kept outside the palace fence and the prince saw
nothing but seducible young women and happy young
men instead. He took part in sports and made music, and the
courtiers arranged parties. One day the prince, curious to
know what happened outside the fence, asked permission
to go out. The king made sure that the prince wouldn't
see anything unpleasant: he arranged a conducted tour,
briefed the carriage driver, told the people around the palace
what to do and what to say, and had the miserable removed.
But the heavenly personages materialised and took the forms
of a beggar, a sick man, a very old man leaning on a stick,
thin as a rake and almost blind, a corpse at the side of the
road, and a wandering monk in a yellow robe. The driver
of the carriage was questioned by the prince. He had to
admit that the world knows a lot of misery, a lot of
suffering.

The prince asked about the wandering monk in the
yellow robe.

'He is a man, your highness, who has given up the
superficial life and who tries to approach reality through
discipline and meditation.'

'So you think there is a reality which is more real than
what I see, and hear, and smell, and feel, and taste, and can
imagine?'

'Yes, your highness.'

'And do you know that reality?'

The coachman didn't know what to say. He did believe
there was a higher reality, but he couldn't say he knew that
reality. The driver was a devout Hindu who believed that

the apparent injustice of earthly suffering is an illusion and that behind, or in front of, or next to that illusion, or perhaps somewhere in the illusion itself, would exist a reality which could explain everything.

'Life is suffering,' Buddha concluded. He wasn't a Buddha then, but Gautama Siddarta, an Indian prince. Even happiness, enjoyment, gaiety are forms of suffering, because these feelings are limited in time, and will stop. The essence of happiness is suffering because we always know that there will be an end to it because the subject, or the person, or the thought which causes happiness is temporary. The energetic businessman who is successful has a heart-attack, the happy couple suddenly apply for a divorce, the promising child falls out with his parents and runs away from home, the fertile pastures are flooded, the ship sinks or is broken up, the loved pet is run over by a car. Everything is temporary, will die, will cease to exist. The baby which is now gurgling and burbling in its cot will die, now or later, but it will die.

What the Indian prince surmised then, has been surmised by everybody. Every human being who reflects, who observes, suspects that life is suffering. Perhaps he doesn't like talking about it and prefers to push the thought away, but he knows that life is a difficult road, a way of the Cross which will continue till it is ended by death. The thought is suppressed by drinking, by work, by spending time on hobbies, but the thought will always return. It is possible to find temporary relief in books, or in conversations with friends, but books begin to bore after a while and friends don't really have an answer either. So doubt returns. If life is suffering, and if death approaches a little more every day, then why live? If Buddhism hadn't gone any further than this first truth, that life and suffering are synonyms, then Buddhism could be called a negative religion, without anyone arguing the point. But there are another three truths, stated by Buddha:

suffering is caused by desire, the desire to have and the desire to be;

26

the desire, the desire to have and the desire to be, can be
broken;
the desire can be broken by applying the eightfold path.

It was a monotonous, rather cheerless trip. Nothing happened.
Three meals a day, a cup of coffee in the morning, tea in the
afternoon. A blue, almost flat sea, tidily enclosed by the horizon
on all sides. I began to long for a gale or a collision, but the only
adventures offered to me were to be found in the Buddhist books
neatly arranged on the shelf in my cabin, one of which I took to
my deckchair every time I set out for the sundeck.

I thought I could understand the Buddhist theory. Life is
suffering. Of course. There is pure suffering, the physical
suffering I remembered from the war years. There is also boredom; I had experienced it at school.

And there is enjoyment, which is spoiled by the knowledge
that it can stop any minute. And happiness, which is so airy that
it is gone before it has touched the spirit. Suffering is perhaps a
big word for someone who has grown up in the heavy porridge-
with-sugar-and-butter atmosphere of Holland, but in a Dutch
streetcar it can easily be spotted, disguised and nicely dressed
to be sure—but it is there.

And this suffering had bothered me, and it had driven me on to
this ship. I had suspected, I still suspected, that suffering could
be explained, and once explained, accepted. But Buddhism went
further than that, it didn't talk about 'explaining' but about
'doing away with'. I wanted to get rid of suffering altogether. I
had tried to find a solution by going to church, by reading about
Christianity, but the dogmas of the Christian faith seemed unacceptable to me—believing something because you had to.

Only when I read the dialogues of Socrates had I begun to see
a little light. The description which Plato gives of the death of
Socrates really cheered me up. The imperturbability with which
he, even at the forced end of his life, remained pleasant, indifferent,
quite detached, fascinated me. But how did he get that way? Plato
doesn't say. I wanted to know what I should *do* to find true
equanimity. It is possible to ascertain that life is suffering, a thesis

which is easy to defend. But to get stuck in a thesis is frustrating, irritating. All right, so we suffer. Then what? How do you stop it? If you continue to think in this direction the result is a circle, and you just go round and round.

Ouspensky and Gurdjieff seemed to point a way but they were both dead when I came across their writings. I found a lot of useful information in a book written by a Hindu master.* But I was looking for something which I could do, here and now. Not a spiritual door I could knock on, but a real door, made of wood, with a live man behind it who would say something I could hear. In Japan there are Buddhist monasteries. Japan is a country easily accessible to westerners. Japan possesses living masters of wisdom, masters who accept disciples. I could have gone to India or Ceylon, but the stories I had heard about youthful idealists who had aimlessly wandered about, to die, in the end, of dysentry, didn't appeal to me. If I got sick in Japan I would be able to find a doctor. There would be Japanese who could speak English. I wouldn't be altogether lost should anything go wrong.

On the ship I re-read Ouspensky's *The Fourth Way*.† He says there are four ways to find the ultimate truth, complete freedom. The way of the fakir is to conquer the physical body, a long, difficult and uncertain way, tried and rejected by Buddha. The way of the monk, a shorter and more certain way, is based on faith; one has to believe strongly before anything can be seen or experienced. The way of the yogi is an intellectual way, the way of thought and consciousness, evoked by certain exercises. And the last is the way of the 'sly' man, the man who doesn't believe in anything but who wants to experience, who looks for proof.

Ouspensky then gives the method applied by the sly man. He always appears to be an ordinary fellow, he doesn't wear a robe or a monk's habit, but he is a member of a group and engages in exercises, at fixed times, regularly, supervised by a teacher.

* Swami Prabhavananda and Christopher Isherwood, *How to Know God* (Allen & Unwin, 1953).
† P. D. Ouspensky, *The Fourth Way* (Routledge & Kegan Paul, 1957).

If I had lived in Japan I might have become a disciple of a teacher without moving into a monastery. Zen masters accept lay disciples who come to see him once a day, always early in the morning, and continue living in the world although they often meditate with the monks and take part in the monasteries' activities. But now that I had a chance, because of an inheritance and lack of responsibilities, to give myself completely to something, I wanted to try and do as much as possible. At least I thought so on the ship, when I was still under the impression that I had a free choice. Now, as I write this, I believe I had no choice at all, and was doing no more than work out the results of causes which were buried somewhere in the past. A man's 'liberty' is quite small. Even when he thinks he is making a choice the result is already fixed. A man can only make tiny decisions. He can decide to get up early and it may be that he will succeed if he keeps trying. He can decide to obey traffic rules and he may succeed again, if he repeats the decision ten times a day. Every change in the daily routine is very difficult, but, fortunately, not impossible. There is freedom in the small things of daily life, and the mystical training is possible when we make use of this freedom. But a big choice, to go or not to go to Japan, is not free.

The ship touched Bombay. I went ashore and couldn't move for beggars. A hungry city. I couldn't budge without being bothered by crowds of small children asking for money or food. The hunger we knew in Holland during the winter of 1944/5 seemed to be a normal and permanent phenomenon here. A sailor told me that he had been in a brothel where women were locked away in iron cages; for a few florins a client could spend five minutes or so in the cage, while his successors waited their turn impatiently behind a curtain of jute bags. The sailor hadn't entered the cage, but had thrown in some money through the bars. According to him it was better in China: everybody dressed in a blue overall and a cap, walking in processions and waving flags and small books, but there was no hunger and no women in cages. I wondered if the women in the cages, and the beggars with their maimed and rotting limbs, would be in a better position if I found enlightenment in Japan. Misery stays. Another clever person is produced, hiding non-transferable wisdom behind a mysterious smile, but hunger and disease and exploitation continue. Misery is perhaps not, most probably not, bound to this planet, but is a cosmic phenomenon, set up in such a big way that actual destruction of suffering is a hopeless task.

On the ship I also read about the theories of karma and reincarnation. Karma is the law of cause and effect, reincarnation the law of rebirth. If I do something wrong in this life I shall be an invalid in my next life, not as a fine, but as an exercise, an extra exercise (as if life as a healthy person isn't difficult enough already) to bring me finally to pure consciousness. The soul has to be chastened, and chastening goes with suffering. In one life the soul cannot be sufficiently purified, so more lives have to be lived, 500 or 600—then enlightenment comes and further lives are lived in other spheres, where there is less suffering and more enjoyment. Also, there is an in-between period, a pause between every death and every rebirth, a sort of holiday for those who have done well and a hell for those who have done badly. When I read about these theories and thought about them they seemed acceptable, but they did not provide a solution.

It could be that the women in the cages of Bombay and the beggars were digesting karma; that would explain suffering, but not the cause of suffering. Why are beings created who have the chance to live in a wrong way and, as a consequence, have to do difficult exercises (like having to live as an invalid) later? I am not even talking now of such harsh ideas as crime and punishment and eternal hell. The Hindu theory is kind and tolerant compared with Christian teaching as it was formulated by the Christian churches a little while ago. The method of Buddha seemed to me in the end, for myself anyway, the best: no questions about the why of everything, but a disregard of doubt, an attempt to do away with being involved with the pain of the world, and a conscious start along a path which has been tried by one man who managed to reach its goal, a path which has been followed by many others who used the original explorer as their guide. A possible path, not a vague theory. A path which still has living guides today, the Buddhist masters. I knew that I would have to content myself with the idea that I could not expect any certainty, not even a firm faith in the masters. It would be a way of trial and error, a hesitating effort, a touch and go affair with, perhaps, a little success sometimes, maybe a glimmering of insight, a slightly deepening understanding.

The ship took me to Singapore and Hong Kong and stayed a few days in each port to load and unload. In every port I went ashore and looked around. In the slums I saw people sleeping in the streets; I had to look where I was going so as not to step on them. There were beggars again, and pathetic children and whores, although there was no comparison with the raw suffering of Bombay. To suffer, and why? Caused by the eternal desire which we carry about with us. We want to have and to increase our possessions continually. We want to be, and to be more, and to continue to be, even after death, through our children or through the name of the firm we founded. We want to have a name, a personality, which has to grow in importance all the time. The desire is mainly subconscious; it keeps us going. We work, we boast, we advertise ourselves, and on every photograph our first concern is to see if our image has come out well. We do not suspect that our body is nothing but an empty shell which will go to the wastepaper basket of the cemetery or crematorium. The ego, the false I, which we carry about with so much trouble and feed continuously, is a little cloud, which changes its shape all the time and consists of snapshots ranging from baby to old man. What concerned us last year is of no importance now, and what concerns us now will be forgotten and senseless next year. But even if we realise this the desire will continue and we shall muddle about in the dark.

Buddhism is not gloomy; only the first truth has a sombre sound. The thirst for life, which pushes us around and keeps us away from ultimate reality, can be broken. The situation isn't hopeless. The destruction of self, as advised by Buddha, is not suicide.

The last stretch of the ship's journey, from Hong Kong to Kobe, was the most difficult, as I had expected. I was alone now, the Danes finally having found their ship in Hong Kong. The daily discipline of reading and writing interrupted by meals couldn't be kept up any longer. I began to wander all over the ship and visit the bar regularly. The monastery was getting very close. It had been a vague shape on the horizon for a long time but now it began to have a very definite outline.

I foresaw a lot of real and imaginary difficulties. I wasn't quite so sure if I wanted to break my ego and give up everything which up till then had had some value for me.

A story told by Ouspensky, which he must have heard from his mysterious teacher, Gurdjieff, an Armenian who graduated from an esoteric school in Tibet, cheered me up considerably. Gurdjieff compares the man who has no answer, who knows of no solution, to a prisoner who spends his time aimlessly in jail.

Now there are prisoners who claim that jail is the only possible place to be in and that there is nothing outside jail. That type of prisoner, Gurdjieff says, should be left alone. They are stupefied, and they don't want to do anything, and as long as they remain in that state of mind they can't be helped.

But there are prisoners who want to escape, who are not content with their surroundings and who suspect that there is a much more attractive area outside their jail. They can't really know this, because they are born in jail, or else the memory which they might have retained of free life has been artificially removed. But they do believe in the possibility of getting out and away, and they believe there is a lot of sense in trying.

But the jail is well guarded, there are towers with searchlights, and trained, ever-alert warders armed with the latest make of machine-gun; and there is a deep moat around the building, filled with sharks and hungry crocodiles. The walls are high, strong and smooth. It is almost hopeless even to think of escape. But it can be done. Prisoners *have* escaped, in groups, well prepared and brilliantly led by masters. The masters know the area outside the jail and can live within as well as outside the jail.

But they can't carry anyone outside; all they can do is point the way and they know all the tricks.

The ship approached Kobe in the early morning. I had got up at dawn so as not to miss anything. There was nobody on deck and the sea around me was empty. All I could see was one small fishing boat. An old Japanese was busy pulling up his nets. He saw me and I waved. He waved back. It seemed a good omen: at least I was welcomed cordially.

Four

Caught between the tigers

Hidden away at the back of the monastery gardens was a cemetery with small pagodas and gravestones, green and covered with moss. On these centuries old tombs, texts were chiselled in Chinese characters. I was sweeping leaves there, preparing heaps to be carted away to another part of the grounds. The head monk had ordered me to 'tidy up', a hopeless task, for the cemetery was neglected and overgrown with weeds. I did what I could and worked at a leisurely pace, secure in the knowledge that, in an hour or so, the kitchen bell would call me for a cup of green tea and a biscuit. The biscuits came from a tin brought that morning by an old lady as her gift to the temple. Every day somebody would bring something, biscuits and sweets, a bag of rice, or steaming noodles, boiled and presented on a wooden tray. These gifts aren't just meant to cheer the monks, but have a deeper meaning: those who offer them are showing that they too believe in the way of Buddha, but that, because of their circumstances or mental constitution, they are not yet ready to take part. They hope that their compassion will enable them to be more active in the next life, to become a monk or a lay-disciple of a master.

That day I had found a kitten in the cemetery, a very thin little animal adorned with a gaily coloured ribbon. I picked it up, got it some water and milk and found it a place in the sun on one of the verandas. A few minutes later the temple dog arrived, a nasty creature which would lie in wait for me and suddenly dart out, snapping and growling. Without the slightest hesitation it rushed at the kitten, seized it by the neck and shook it till it was dead.

People from around the temple would often leave kittens in the garden. They wouldn't kill the animals because that didn't suit their religion; Buddha is compassionate and to kill is cruel. By taking them to a monastery garden they transferred the cats' souls to Buddha and his monks. Meanwhile the monks were stuck with the helpless kittens and their doleful mewing. Usually the dog took care of them and if he wasn't around the monks drowned them in the pool, at night, when nobody was about. Without being aware of it, I had dropped my broom and leant against a tomb. I was crying. I hadn't cried in years.

A car came past with a loudspeaker attached to its roof broadcasting a loud march. The music was interrupted and a healthy hypnotic voice told me about the wonderful pain-absorbing effect of aspirin or some similar drug.

I had been in Japan long enough to understand a little Japanese. The newness of the exotic, mystical Far East had gone. Perhaps the people here looked different and sometimes wore outlandish clothes; and it was a fact that I was living in one of 8000 temples dedicated to the higher spheres, and true, of course, that I was daily admitted to a wise, and probably all-enlightened master. Even so, I couldn't rid myself of the clear and painful feeling that nothing had changed.

That I cried did not surprise me. I was amazed, rather, that I had not fallen into the pit of despair earlier. There were no thoughts along the lines of 'why did I involve myself in all this' or 'this will never lead to anything'. I was just sad, without having to describe or define the feeling. Later that day, while sitting in the meditation hall, I reflected that I had trouble fitting in, that I felt like a chicken which has to live with ducklings, that I could not connect, could not communicate. The definition wasn't very satisfactory. It was more than that; after all, I had been in strange environments before. I felt, not isolated, but hopeless. I saw no way out. This was the end of the world—I couldn't go any further. I didn't want to go back so I had to stay. There was no rebellion in me—I wasn't against anything at all. But I did feel ridiculous: here was the tough rider of motorcycles, the seducer of sweet and innocent girls, the reader of deep and intellectual books, the guerilla fighter in eternal combat with the establishment, crying against a tomb in a deserted monastic garden.

Peter has told me that a man plays many parts, and *none* of these parts is real. Every part is another mask, unconsciously formed by environment and aptitude. A man is like an onion. When he goes into himself, by meditation and other exercises, by discipline, by fighting his 'self', the layers of the onion drop away, one by one, till the last layer disappears and nothing remains. I didn't like the last part of this explanation: nothing isn't much. Why go to all that trouble to become nothing at all, to dissolve into a vacuum? 'But then,' I said, 'one is no longer there. And if one is no longer there there is nothing left to enjoy the great insight, the immeasurable liberty.'

'Look at the master,' Peter said, 'there he is. You see?' The master happened to be passing by and we watched him enter the gate. Peter laughed, not an ecstatic laugh, veiling secrets, but a merry laugh, a pleasant, gay 'ha ha'.

'Yes,' I said. But I didn't understand. Yet I did understand. I felt he was right. I knew too that I would know one day, know clearly and without any doubt, that he had uttered a tremendous truth. That everything had to be destroyed, given up, every pride, every jealousy, every security, every hook or projection which the personality can grab and hang on to.

An American lady once said to the master that she, deep down in her mind or soul, possessed a holy kernel in which she could find peace, and that this kernel was always with her, sometimes hard to reach but in any case present.

'Yes,' the master said, 'that causes you a lot of trouble, that kernel—it's in your way. Give it up, whatever idea you have of it. Get rid of it!'

I think, from the way she reacted, that she felt very well what he meant, but to feel something is not the same as to know it, to be able to apply it. She left the monastery complete with kernel, as I had leant against the tomb, complete with sadness.

About that time I was told the famous story about the man who falls. He is hanging above an abyss, clinging to a thin branch of a tree growing between the rocks. He may, with some effort, be able to pull himself up, but there is a ferocious

tiger there, growling and showing his teeth. If he lets go,
he'll fall into the claws of another tiger waiting below.
And while he hangs there and worries, two mice come along,
a white mouse and a black mouse, and start nibbling through
the branch, his only security. Anybody who 'studies' Zen
will, at some time, get into a similar position. He is sure that
he has to do something, to give something up. He cannot
refuse to do something because the position he happens to
be in is disastrous. But whatever he does will not improve
matters. And while he hesitates and worries, the mice of
'yes' and 'no', 'this' or 'that', 'good' and 'bad' nibble away.

It isn't a bad story, but even with stories one must be very careful.
Some men are professional story-collectors. I met one of them, a
writer, greedily gathering more and more stories, anecdotes, juicy
bits. That way all you'll have is a book full of jokes.

In the monastery, stories were scarce. The training accentuated
meditation and the importance of the *koan*. The master always
asked the same question: What is your answer? He had given me
the *koan*, and I had to find an answer to the problem. Every
morning when I visited him he expected the answer—he seemed
completely convinced that I would give it to him, on that particular morning, at that very moment. It would have to bubble up,
somewhere out of myself.

He wasn't prepared to give me a hint or to lead the way. The
first *koan* is important, it is the gateless gate, the closed opening
through which the pupil has to fight his way in (or out). He has
to do it himself. And the fight is his meditation, his daily discipline, the change in the way he looks at things, in his own being.
When the master gave instruction it was about the technique of
meditation, about how to concentrate. 'Become one with your *koan*,
forget yourself, forget everything which is connected with you.
When you are sitting there, sit still, in balance, breathe quietly,
destroy everything in your mind and repeat your *koan* as if your
life depends on it, quietly, over and over again. Don't rush yourself, don't get excited, but stay calm and indifferent, indifferent to
anything which worries you, or seems important, or fascinates.'

'That's difficult,' I would say.

'Of course it is difficult,' the master said. 'Do you think it wasn't difficult for me? I used to visit my master every day, as you do now, and I was a very slow fellow. For two years I mucked about with the *koan* without getting anywhere and then I had to go to China because the army wanted me.'

'Yes?' I asked, surprised. 'But you are a Buddhist. Buddhists aren't allowed to kill, are they?'

'Allowed, allowed,' the master said, 'I had to. If I had refused I would have been shot. But in the army, in Manchuria, I meditated a lot. I was always doing guard duty; the other soldiers were very fond of me for I took their duty as well. Look, like this.'

He got up and stood there, on his platform, a little old man in a Buddhist robe, and stretched his body until he was rigid and fierce, to attention. 'This was my rifle, I had my arm out like this. And then I concentrated on the *koan* which my master had given me, for hours and hours on end. You can meditate while you are standing up—it isn't quite as good as when you are sitting in the lotus position, but it can be done. Of course you have to be careful that you don't fall over, but I always had a rifle to lean on.'

'And did you solve your *koan*?'

'Not then,' he said. 'Later, when I was back in Japan and had become a monk again. I began to understand and it didn't interest me any more to prove my understanding to the master. I visited him again every morning and during one of those visits he nodded. He immediately gave me the next *koan*, an easy one.'

'And you said nothing to your master?'

'No, why should I have said anything? I knelt and kept quiet, as I had been quiet so often,'

'So there was no laughing, or shouting, nobody hit anyone?'

'You have read too much,' the master said. 'I told you you shouldn't read so much. You identify yourself with all sorts of heroes and fools and try to swallow their experiences. It isn't wrong to read, but it shouldn't lead to dreaming, or living through another person.'

The conversations with the teacher were laborious. He tried

to use words which he thought I knew. Sometimes I returned mumbling from such a visit and tried to remember the words I hadn't understood, so that I could look them up in my dictionary. Most times we didn't say much to each other. I came in, recited my *koan* and looked at him. He would wait for a few seconds, pick up his small bell and shake it. The bell was my cue to leave. I knew I could grab the bell and that then he wouldn't be able to send me away unless I returned it to him. The bell is always next to the teacher, within reach of the pupil. Should the disciple think that the master doesn't pay enough attention to him he can, in this way, force the issue. I never made use of it. I didn't think I could bully the teacher into sharing his insight with me.

It is a tradition in Zen that no one ever reveals the *koan* he is working on, it is a secret between teacher and pupil: not a very strong tradition, for I discovered that discussing *koans* was a popular pastime to the monks. They made a status game out of it. 'Which *koan* are you on? I have already reached such and such a *koan*.' One would think that such childish boasting must mean a total lack of real insight. I am not sure whether this is true. Most of the monks are sent to the temple by their parents. They have to stay three years and will then graduate to a priesthood and be sent to head a Zen temple somewhere. The organisation is similar to that of the Catholic Church. The monk will then be somebody in his own right, no longer a slave of the master or head monk. He can start to use his training and do social work, he can take charge of temple services, listen to the troubles of his flock. He can supply peace and quiet to those who look for it, for Zen temples and gardens are designed to provide a soothing influence. He can teach meditation and organise groups. He is even allowed to marry. But the comparative status and luxury which waits for him at the end of the three years' monastic training is not enough to pull him through. There must be another stimulus. The teacher cannot let him sit and muddle with the *koan* for too long, so when he shows some insight, even if it is very little, the teacher may pass him. The voluntary monk and the layman are a different kettle of fish; they do things the hard way. A priest who returns to the monastery, after some years of playing the part of priest, will find his teacher rather different from what he remembers.

But forced or voluntary, the monastery's schedule is the same. Each disciple starts off with one of the 'big' *koans*. He may get the Mu *koan*, an extraordinary story about a monk who asks his teacher whether a puppy-dog, who happens to be around, has the Buddha nature as well: a senseless question to any Buddhist, because Buddha said that everything has Buddha nature, so the puppy cannot be an exception. The teacher answers by saying 'Mu'. Mu means no, nothing, emptiness, denial of everything. The monk doesn't understand and is told to meditate on the word Mu. His training has started. Another 'big' *koan* is: Everybody knows the sound of two clapping hands. Now what is the sound of one clapping hand? A third *koan* is: Show me the face you had before your parents were born. Show me your original face.

All *koans* are illogical and go beyond the reasoning mind. The monk may try to give a sensible answer, but if he doesn't it will be just the same: the master will ring his bell and the monk has to leave the room.

The answers which, after many years of hard work, despair and near insanity, may be accepted, will be diverse. Perhaps the monk will make a nonsensical remark; maybe he laughs, or looks at the teacher in a peculiar way or does something, like knocking on the floor or waving. If the master nods, the next *koan* will follow, to deepen the monk's insight. There are rows and rows of *koans*, and the monk who solves them all has to leave the monastery to practise his insight in the world, perhaps as a teacher, perhaps as an inconspicuous civilian. Only very few disciples come to the end of the road, which doesn't matter, for the monastery is not a school intended to produce nothing but masters. Everybody is required to do what he can, and the teacher helps, quietly, often passively, sometimes by force. If you do anything at all, do it well. Don't look at the result. The result is important, did you say? Don't talk nonsense.

Five

A large glass of soya sauce and a dangerous snake

A man who has got himself through a whole day without having learned anything and who goes to bed as stupid as he got up, is a dead man. I think I found this bit of wisdom in an American book, a book on success in business. The moral of the story is that you must be aware, because you can make a lot of money that way.

I didn't like the book. Why is it so important to be successful, to make a profit? Isn't it true that success and profit are illusions without substance? Whatever has a beginning will end.

A negative, destructive way of thinking, a part of my personality at that time, had entered the monastery gate. The result was that I was not very conscious, not particularly attentive to the situations in which I took part; and I didn't know I was not attentive. I dreamt a lot.

The head monk described my state of mind even more exactly. 'You are asleep,' he said, 'you are snoring.'

We were in the kitchen. I was cleaning vegetables, rather carelessly. The head monk asked me to stop mucking about and to follow him. He took me to the room reserved for visitors. There was a low table with a teapot, a tin of bitter powdered green tea and a piece of bamboo, cut into the shape of a shaving-brush. He had asked me to bring a kettle of boiling water and I poured this onto the green powder. He whipped the tea with the brush till it foamed. Kneeling we each drank a cup and then he looked at me.

'Buddha,' said the head monk 'had to go a long way before he found the final enlightenment. Later he told others about the road he followed so that they would be able to follow him.

Buddha talked a lot about right awareness. Do you know what it is?'

I tried to shift my weight, for my legs were already beginning to hurt again. 'Looking where you are going,' I said.

'Yes,' the head monk said, 'but you can't do that when you are asleep. When you are asleep anything can happen and you won't even know about it. The temple may burn down and when you eventually wake up because your sleeping bag is getting burnt, it will be too late. Don't take me literally. The monastic training tries to wake us up, but when it is time to sleep you may sleep. But when you are not asleep, be awake. When you are cleaning vegetables, you really have to clean them. The idea is to throw the good pieces into the pot and the rotten pieces into the tin, not the other way around. Whatever you do, do it well, as well as you can, and be aware of what you are doing. Don't try to do two things at the same time, like pissing and cleaning your teeth. I have seen you do that. Perhaps you think you are saving time that way, but the result is no more than a mess in the lavatory and a mess in your mouth.'

'And where do I get by being aware?'

The head monk shrugged, and dropped his eyelids.

'I don't care where it gets you. I am merely advising you to stay awake. We, the teacher and the monks and the other disciples of the master, can't help you much. To stay awake is self discipline. We can force you, in a way, to meditate, but we can't make you concentrate on your *koan*. You are free to work on your problem, while you are perched on your cushions, or to dream away.'

'Right,' I said, 'I'll try it. I'll try to stay awake.'

'Try,' the head monk said, 'what a word! You mustn't try, you must just do it.'

Zen monks don't indulge in long conversations so I began to get up.

'Wait a minute,' the head monk said. 'I want to warn you. If ever you succeed in waking up a bit, be careful that it doesn't go to your head. We used to have a monk here who really did his best to be aware of every situation. When, after three years, he became a priest, the master sent him to a small temple up North.

After a while a young man came to keep him company. This young man intended to join a monastery but he wanted to try the life in a temple first, because the routine is different from ours. Temple-priests and monks don't get up as early as we do, they meditate less or not at all, and they are not in contact with a master. The priest tried to teach the young man as much as possible and used all sorts of daily events as examples.'

> One day there was an earthquake, quite a strong earthquake and part of the temple caved in. When the earthquake stopped the teacher said: 'Look, now you have been able to see how a Zen man behaves under stress. You will have noticed that I didn't panic. I was quite aware of what was happening. I took you by the arm and we went to the kitchen, because that is the strongest part of the temple. I was proved right because the kitchen is still in one piece and we have survived the earthquake—we aren't even wounded. That I, in spite of my self-control and awareness, did suffer a slight shock, you may have deduced from the fact that I drank a large glass of water, something I would never do under normal circumstances.'
>
> The young man didn't say anything but smiled.
>
> 'What's so funny?' the priest asked.
>
> 'That wasn't water, reverend Sir,' the young man said, 'that was a very large glass of soy sauce.'

The day the head monk lectured me I became ill. I got diarrhoea, probably because of the seaweed we had for dinner that evening, a Japanese delicacy of which we had each eaten a bowlful.

I missed part of the evening meditation because I couldn't stay in the same place for twenty-five minutes. I had to get up in the middle of a period, bow to the head monk, explain my predicament in a whisper, and rush out of the hall without bowing to the statue of Manjusri, the fierce Bodhisatva who specialises in sword rattling. In emergencies even Zen training will make exceptions.

That night, around 2.0 a.m., I got up for the umpteenth time, to go to the lavatory. The court was lit by the moon and just in front of the small building which housed the toilets I saw a snake, a fat snake, coiled up, about twelve feet long. Its head pointed in my direction and its split tongue flicked in and out coldly, evilly. I shouted and rushed off towards the main temple. On the way I tripped over something and fell. The fall woke me up a little and I considered that panic might be unnecessary, since the snake wasn't following me. I stopped but then rushed off again. The head monk looked at me, and covered his mouth with his hand. He was a Japanese of the artistocratic type, lanky and well-formed, with a beautiful thin curved nose and calm, wide, and slanting eyes. His even, sparkling white teeth had amazed me, as most monks had irregular teeth, haphazardly placed, yellow and filled in with metal. The sparkling white teeth were now in a glass on the table and I looked the other way while he completed his face.

'A snake,' I said, panting. 'A big fat dangerous snake. Near the toilets. If we are quick we may catch it and kill it.'

The head monk gave me a shy grin while he snapped his teeth into place. 'Never mind,' he said. 'Let the snake be. We have had him for years. He catches rats and he lives in the courtyard. I should have warned you. Just walk around him, he is harmless.'

The snake even had a name which I have forgotten now. Something with 'chan' at the end. 'San' means 'mister' and goes after the names of grown-up human beings. Children and pets have 'chan' after their names. I was very annoyed with myself when I got back to my room. Nothing is important enough to become upset about. I should have known that. I shouldn't need monastic training to be aware of such a home truth. Nothing, nothing at all. I didn't get upset in the old days when I had a flat tyre on my motorcycle, did I? Or if I lost one of my favourite books? So why get upset now because I found a snake in my way? And why should I be upset about having got upset? Instead of getting more detached this training was making me nervous, hysterical. 'Idiot!' 'Unbelievably stupid fool!' For days I called myself names, often aloud, even in the meditation hall. The head monk had to shout at me. 'Stay awake,' he shouted.

In those days I found several possibilities of making life more enjoyable. We had entered a period of 'soft training', which meant we were getting up at 4 a.m. instead of 3 a.m., meditation in the afternoon was cancelled, some monks were on leave, visiting their parents in the country and the teacher had gone to Tokyo to lecture. Of the three older monks who, together, ran the monastery, two were away, so that the head monk was kept busy and we hardly saw him. In the morning he gave us instructions for the entire day and after that he disappeared. I helped to cut wood and dig the gardens, in the afternoon I studied Japanese and only in the evening did I meditate with the others, supervised by a young monk who shortened the periods and ignored wobbling, moving about and falling asleep. At first I had washed my own clothes, a job I didn't like, and now I bought two pairs of jeans and a pile of underwear and shirts. The shop didn't stock my size but they took the order, and within a few days a neat parcel was delivered to my room, at 10 per cent discount. Now that I had more clothes, I could afford to save up my laundry and take it, once a week, to a washerwoman around the corner. I also found another restaurant; the first, where I had gone on doctor's prescription, didn't have enough variety in the menu. But my most important discovery was the public bathhouse. In the monastery the monks were only allowed to have a bath every ninth day; they could have a shower whenever they wanted, but the shower was cold. The monastery's bathhouse was small and contained an iron bath which was heated by a small fire, to be fed with leaves and twigs only. Forests are scarce in Japan and firewood is a luxury. A monk had to spend the best part of a day heating the bath and when he finally managed to get it to the right temperature the master would go first and then the monks in order of importance. I would always be the last one, as I was the last arrival in the monastery. That didn't mean I had to sit in dirty water, because the Japanese clean themselves before they get into the tub, splashing about with basins and lots of soap before finally immersing themselves in the hot water, relaxing their weary bones and muscles till the next person begins to show open signs of impatience.

The bathhouse I found was a larger, more luxurious version

of what I had got used to in the monastery. I had to walk for a few minutes through the narrow streets of the area, past the small shops and streetstands, and I was greeted by everyone. Everybody knew me: there were only twenty-nine westerners in Kyoto then, and more than a million Japanese. I would give ten cents to the lady at the entrance and undress on a sort of balcony in the hall, where not only the lady at the door but everybody who went in or out as well, could see me. The women were very interested. A white man, apparently, was a welcome change, and although they must have seen a lot of details in the cinema, this live show was more fascinating. Three dimensions are better than two.

I used to go in the early afternoon and soak as long as possible in the large, swimming-pool sized bath, lined with beautifully glazed tiles. Bathing used to be mixed, but since the American occupation new ideas influenced local behaviour and now men and women were separated. I got to know the other regulars after a while and began to greet the old men, who came every afternoon, by name. 'Hello Jan-san.' they would say. 'Hello Tanaka-san, hello Kobori-san, hello Sasaki-san. Nice water to-day.' And then we would groan together contentedly. I had more contact with the old men than with the monks. They asked me how long I had to meditate every evening. 'Three hours,' I said proudly. 'And in a little while, when the master is back, another two hours in the afternoon. And another hour again in the morning.' They shook their heads compassionately and nodded at each other, admiringly. They really had a strange friend now.

'And don't your legs hurt?'

'Sure,' and I indicated all the painful spots.

The monastery didn't object, although the head monk must have known exactly what I was doing.

Six

A thirsty fish

While studying the head monk's daily behaviour I gradually began to distinguish various characteristics. Of these his equanimity impressed me most. He, rather than the master, was the example which I used in my routine. I think he knew that he was serving as an example, not only for me, but for anybody who was connected with the monastery. In these esoteric disciplines it is very dangerous to identify with another person, because if the other does anything which, in the eyes of the imitator, cannot be accepted or justified, the example comes tumbling down and breaks into a thousand pieces; and with the example, the image, the god, the whole discipline, breaks and appears senseless. Perhaps awareness of this process forced the head monk to avoid any spectacular behaviour. He obeyed the monastic rules strictly and got up earlier than the others. He went to bed later. During meditation he never moved at all, he struck the bell exactly on time, and during the communal meals he seemed to watch all his own moves. Still, there was nothing stiff about him. He slipped through life easily; he was free, kind, quiet, perhaps even careless or indifferent. Nothing touched him. When I tried to start a conversation with him, he would listen for a few moments and then bring me back to whatever I happened to be doing. If *he* wanted to talk he would choose the moment and the environment. He created situations, quite a tricky art to master.

That under his strict correctness another quality was hidden, I could deduce from the expression in his eyes. Indifference is an unpleasant word, so perhaps one should say 'detachment'. One could see that he was really quite free, but that, even so, he did show interest in others and in any activity he might be engaged in for the moment. He had an attractive gait, as if he walked on soft but very strong springs, springs which he could control completely. If he had accentuated his way of walking just a little it would have been silly, affected, but it wasn't. So right that it is almost wrong: an essential part of Zen.

When I met him his formal Zen training, the *koan* study, had finished. He didn't visit the master any more to demonstrate his progress (or lack of progress) as we did, but he was in constant touch with the teacher. We, the disciples, had to visit the master every day, in the uncomfortable early hours, to struggle with the *koan* and find the hidden opening which is no opening. He was in.

When we left the meditation hall to visit the master, the head monk would stay in his place, quietly, his eyes fixed on the floor. If the rule had been applied strictly he would have been out of the monastery, because once a disciple has solved the last *koan* he should not be permitted to live at the community's expense. Every penny which is received by the monastery comes as a gift, either directly because somebody has presented a few notes or a cheque in a closed envelope, or through begging, because the monks never miss a day. Each morning they walk through the streets of the city, holding the begging bowl, and waiting patiently till somebody will give—they never approach people in the street. They shout HOOOOO! to catch people's attention, and often it is difficult for the passerby to catch up with the monk and present his gift for the monks concentrate on their 'Ho' and appear to be in a daze.

I think that the master hadn't sent the head monk away because he needed him. The master had to watch his own health, which was weak because of a slight stroke a few years back, and the energy of the head monk must have been welcome.

I was told, later, how the head monk had come to Zen. He was the only son of a couple of which both man and wife were medical practitioners. The parents had spoiled him; they were well off and not often at home. He had a scooter of the more expensive type, was a member of sports clubs, had a number of rooms in the house reserved for him and two servants to look after his needs.

A car accident killed both parents at the same moment. He was sixteen years old at the time and the shock must have been severe. A mental breakdown and attempts at suicide followed, but as a point of light or a rock to lean on he had the Zen master, whom he knew because his father had taken him to the temple, of which he was an active member. The father even used to come for meditation and join the monks in the hall from time to time. When he came to see the master to discuss his parents' death he was rebellious. He didn't want to ask the teacher anything, he merely wanted to tell him that life on earth makes no sense and knows no justice. Why should he, a sixteen-year-old boy, suddenly have to lose his parents? Why was he born? If everything will stop and be destroyed why consent to partake in any activity, why live?

'Yes,' the master said, and allowed the boy to go home. But he kept coming back till the master lost his patience. 'If you only come here to complain you may as well stay at home. What do you want of me?'

'I want,' the boy said 'to know why I must suffer. I want you to tell me.'

'I won't tell you anything,' the teacher said. 'You know the answer yourself. And if you like, you can tell *me* the answer.'

'I understand what you are telling me,' the boy said. 'I will have to become a monk and you will give me a *koan*, and then I will have to meditate and repair my own clothes and have a bath once every nine days. Now why should I do that? My karma, the result of whatever I did during previous lives, is good. I am rich, I own a large house. I am intelligent, I can go to the university and become a doctor as my parents did. I can have girl friends and have children and my children will be well off too. Why should I give it all up to find out something which, you say, I already know?'

'Well, don't then', the master said. 'I never told you to become a monk. You can do what you like. But I don't want you to come here any more; I am a busy man and I can't help you.'

'But if I do become a monk you will have time for me? Then you will help me to reach the point which, according to you, I have already reached?'

'I suppose I'll have to,' the master said, 'but you are like a fish saying it is thirsty.'

So he did eventually become a monk, but he ran away three times and returned three times. The *koan* must have given him a lot of trouble because after some years he had to adopt extreme methods. He didn't go to bed any more but kept on meditating, on a rock in the garden, with a bucket of water next to him so that he could splash water into his face to keep himself awake.

When I knew him there were no signs left of erratic behaviour. I couldn't even imagine that this quiet, energy-generating man had ever been a spoiled neurotic boy. I told the master that this complete change was really like a reincarnation in one life. The master shook his head. 'You should forget about reincarnation,' he said. 'In Hinduism there is a lot of talk about the Atman, the divine self which never changes. It lives many lives and comes closer to its God-like core with every new existence on earth so that, after many purifications, it will live its final life on earth before it finds Nirvana, the only real heaven, the sphere of God himself. But Buddhism doesn't attach itself to any theory, not even to the doctrine of the God-like self. Everything, you will find, is illusion, temporary, beyond our reach, and that includes the divine self. Nothing exists, nothing has ever existed, and nothing will ever exist. But when one starts thinking logically, and every time you try to think you are using logic, we think of "this" or "that", and when we think of "nothing" we immediately oppose it, contrast it with "something". Then we imagine an emptiness, and we get stuck in this emptiness. A neurotic boy becoming a balanced man is an interesting process to watch, but without significance. That a man lives many lives, and that all lives are connected and flow into each other, is nice to know. But we, in this monastery, are not engaged in psychiatric treatment, and neither are we a school of philosophy. If you are interested in eastern philosophy and religion, if you want to study reincarnation and karma, you can go through the gate, turn left twice and right three times and you will find yourself in the university of Kyoto. There are professors over there who will be able to answer all your questions, but when you analyse the answers, they will be questions again. The intellect is a beautiful instrument and has a purpose, but here you will discover a different instrument. When you solve *koans* you will have answers which are no longer questions.'

'Yes,' I said, 'that's what I want. Insight.'

The master looked at me kindly.

'Insight, by itself, is of no significance either. I want you to *show* me your insight.'

On the way to the bathhouse I met a Catholic priest, a Jesuit from Germany who taught at a Catholic school for Japanese. The monks had pointed him out to me before, when he walked by but I had never met him. That day he stopped and asked me how I liked the monastery. I was, in those days, well on the way to becoming a fanatical Buddhist because the more I understood about Buddhism, or thought I understood, the more I was convinced that this was the only right way, the most enlightened and effective religion which I had ever encountered. And if the Buddhists are right, I thought, then the others are all wrong and especially the Christians with their ideas about heaven and hell, with their God and Son of God and their definitions of crime and punishment. This celibate Catholic priest who suddenly faced me in the street seemed a clown to me, a very lost soul. Why should he do without sex all his life if he was living in a body meant and equipped for sex? Why should he believe in, dogmas because someone in Italy claimed they were true? No, I thought, I am better than that. I am allowed, I am even compelled, to find out everything for myself, and I only believe and accept what I can believe and accept, and if tomorrow some new insight grows in me I will believe something different tomorrow. I am celibate because I promised to stay away from sex for a certain period, like a man training for a boat race will not smoke for a few weeks. Christ, a hazy man from a far past, is, to this priest, the great Messiah, the saviour, the prophet of a message in which he has to believe unconditionally. Buddha may be another hazy man from a far past but he had no pretensions. He merely said that there is a solution to all human problems and that this solution

can be found by living in a certain way, by meditation, by awareness, by being awake.

Christ always talked about his Father, about God. Buddha
never denied the existence of God but he never confirmed it either.
That is much more reasonable; why should we try to understand
something we'll never be able to understand? It is more practical
to try and reach a certain point, consciously, where insight is
possible and to restrict all attempts to reach enlightenment to the
daily discipline.

I pitied the priest, a man working for a competing business, a
company without a future, a church destined to disappear. I
would have liked to convert him.

The Jesuit didn't show that he felt anything of my hostile
compassion. He seemed very impressed when I told him how
difficult and trying the Zen training is.

'That isn't much!' he said, 'four hours' sleep a night!'

I was told, later, that the training in Jesuit monasteries is
about the same, as far as the daily routine is concerned, as Zen
training. Jesuits hit themselves with a piece of rope. Zen monks
hit each other with a stick. Both methods hurt. I often met the
priest after that but I never risked another conversation. People
who knew him well said that he was a very modest man. He was
reputed to be a graduate twice over, and his lectures were supposed to be brilliant. He meditated at least two hours every day
and often much more because when the school was closed for
holidays or weekends he would retire to his room and could
only be reached when he was needed. The monks considered him
a holy man and when he visited the monastery he wasn't received
by the head monk but by the master himself in his private room.

It seems that in Hokkaido, the northern island of Japan,
there is a small Zen monastery where the master is illiterate.
The teacher was a farmer's son and he had been taken to the
temple when he was very young. He had never learned to
read or write but he completed the *koan* study and came
to complete enlightenment.

That there were other religions except Buddhism he

scarcely realised, until he hear the monks discussing Christianity.

One of his monks had been to the university of Tokyo and the teacher asked him to explain Christianity.

'I don't know much about it,' the monk said, 'but I will bring you the holy book of the Christian religion.'

The master sent the monk to the nearest city and the monk returned with the Bible.

'That's a thick book,' the master said, 'and I can't read. But you can read something to me.'

The monk knew the Bible and read the Sermon on the Mount. The more he read, the more the master was impressed. 'That is beautiful,' he kept saying. 'That is very beautiful.' When the monk finished the sermon the master said nothing for a while. The silence lasted so long that the monk put the Bible down, got himself into the lotus position, and started meditating. 'Yes,' the teacher said finally. 'I don't know who wrote that, but whoever he was, he was either a Buddha or a Bodhisatva. What you read there is the essence of everything I have been trying to teach you here.'

Seven

A difference of rank and a pigeon's egg

Zen is free; Zen training is not. The training is bound to time and place, and tied up with customs and tradition.

Sunday was a special day in the monastery. Then the local people would arrive, neatly dressed, father first, then mother, then the children. At the gate they were welcomed by a bowing monk. When I saw that for the first time, I remembered my early youth: the Free Dutch Reformed Church in Rotterdam and all those devout faces. All week everybody had messed about, but now they marched in, arranged in neat rows, faces folded in just the right expression, bodies tucked away in Sunday suits. History repeats itself; the repetition is unavoidable.

Still, there was a difference. Here festivities started with a drum solo. On the veranda of the main temple there was a drum as big as a beer-barrel, on its side, supported by wooden trestles. Every Sunday morning at nine o'clock, if the monastery wasn't closed because of special exercises for the monks, Gi-san, the monastery's drummer, would give a short rattle on the drum. When the rattle exploded through the gardens I stopped, because this was far too good to miss. At that time it was very quiet in the monastery and also in the surrounding neighbourhood. The rattle, therefore, would be sudden, clear and penetrating, and I could feel it go right through my spine. After a pause of ten to fifteen seconds the drum would start again, slowly working up an easy but impressive rhythm handled by a relaxed Gi-san for he had lots of time—the solo took at least ten minutes. He wouldn't just hit the skin of the drum but would also use the sides of the barrel and cause a hissing rustling sound by stirring his sticks on the drum. I thought that Gi-san must be a master on the instrument but when he happened to be away one Sunday, another monk, haphazardly selected, proved to be just as good.

During the solo the monks entered the temple, where the master was already seated on a large chair, a chair with a back he didn't use since he always sat in the lotus position keeping his back straight without any need for support. The master dressed, for such occasions, in a glorious robe of embroidered silk and brocade. The head monk would sit at his left side, small and inconspicuous on the floor, with a small bell in his hand, and Ke-san, a tall, very thin monk, a temple priest who, years ago, had given up his easy life to become a disciple of the master again, sat in a small fortress consisting of three gongs: a small gong, a middle-sized gong, and an enormous gleaming monster-gong.

When Gi-san gave his final stroke on the drum outside Ke-san hit his gong in the temple, and at that signal the monks' choir started the first *sutra* of Buddha, a rhythmical musical droning of syllables, regularly interrupted by the gongs and bell of their leaders.

I sat uncomfortably among the monks. It would have been better if I could have joined in the chanting but I can't sing, and even if I had had the right voice I wouldn't have been able to remember the words and sounds. That I couldn't read the Chinese characters of the text didn't help much either. The flock sat at the other side of the large temple room and I could feel their curious eyes prick into my body. My larger size and curly brown hair must have contrasted strangely with the small, uniformly bald monks around me.

The chanting lasted a long time, about half an hour, and after that the master would speak: an official sermon within the tradition of Japanese Zen. He would tell stories about the lives of former masters, or would read us something about the life of the Buddha. His voice was monotonous, droning away, and the monks would fall asleep. When one falls asleep in the lotus position the upper part of the body begins to sway, slowly to the front, slowly to the back. Because I couldn't manage to sit properly in balance I couldn't fall asleep either. If I did, I fell over, and I did fall over once, much to the amusement of the flock which immediately emitted a high titter. After that I did everything possible to stay awake. When the sermon was over the head monk hit his bell, the monks woke up with a sudden shock, the gongs began to vibrate all around us, and outside Gi-san started on his drum again.

After that there was a feast and we had to run about carrying large trays filled with red lacquer bowls heaped full of rice and vegetarian soup. I had to help in the kitchen on such occasions, when all cooking pots would be in use and the cook and his assistants slaved away, sweating and feverish, to feed some 100 guests. At washing-up time all the monks worked together and even the master would join in, dressed in his old overalls and with a piece of cloth wrapped around his bald skull to keep the sweat from running into his eyes.

The head monk told me that the master, fifteen years ago, just after the end of the war, had come to the monastery and had lived there alone for two years. He had lived contentedly and quietly, using only a small part of the large building. In the vegetable garden he only ploughed two small fields, and every morning he swept the path to the temple's main entrance. He had meditated alone in the large dusty hall, and when the first monks came he hadn't been excited, just as he hadn't been sad when he was alone.

The monastery was now almost filled to capacity and we even had a new arrival, a young American poet with a beard and tufted eyebrows: Gerald, a professional beatnik from the western United States. I was upset when I found out that Gerald spoke Japanese fluently and knew all the customs of the monastery. I should have enjoyed showing him around and explaining it all to him, from my superior status as a recognised and accepted disciple of the master. But it was the other way round and Gerald treated me in a rather offhand manner. This turned out to be his second visit to the monastery. Some time before he had spent a year in the temple and now he had returned, after a tour of the Far East. He bought a beautiful, brand new, heavy Japanese motorcycle, rented rooms in the north of the city, near the large Biwa lake. He came every morning for *sanzen*, the formal interview with the master, and every evening he joined us for meditation. When we had *sesshins* he spent them in the monastery. At times the gate of the monastery would be closed for a week, the telephone cut and the mail held up. Every year the monastery has at least six *sesshins*, each lasting seven days. Everything is made even more difficult than usual, every rule is applied and the master receives his disciples from three to five times a day. For the duration of the next *sesshin* Gerald got a room next to mine.

With his arrival an extraordinary problem was created. When the master received his disciples we did not go directly from the meditation hall to the master's house, but knelt in a row on one of the verandas of the main temple. We did have a roof above our heads on the veranda but it wasn't a pleasant place because the wind had free play with us, and in winter, in particular, we were very uncomfortable. We knelt on a hard wooden floor, and when the master rang his bell the monk at the head of the queue would get up, bow in the direction of the teacher's house, and go to him, walking along another veranda and up a garden path covered by a narrow roof. Meanwhile the queue moved up one place. There were fifteen monks and four lay disciples, a Japanese woman, a Japanese painter who lived on the premises, Gerald and myself. Peter was an irregular guest. I believe that he had come to the end of his formal training and that the normal rules no longer applied to him. What really happened around me was never very clear because, although I could ask as many questions as I liked, the master, the head monk and Peter, the only authorities I was in contact with, only told me what suited them and that wasn't much.

As the last arrival I had the last place in the queue on the veranda, and sometimes I sat there for an hour or more, kneeling on the wooden boards with burning knees. Every time the queue moved I could shift my limbs, but while the next monk spent his time with the master I would be stuck again, my legs cramped and full of pins and needles. The only remedy I could find was to try push-ups so that my knees were off the floor but this exercise was also rather fatiguing and made my arms and shoulders hurt.

The day Gerald arrived in the monastery he came to see me and said that he would take my place in the queue. It was logical, he said. After all, he had been a disciple of the master before anyone had ever heard of me. The monks, of course, were higher in rank than we were, they had to go first, but of the lay disciples he was more important and senior to me.

'Certainly,' I said. It didn't matter much whether my legs hurt on the veranda or inside in the hall where we returned after the interview with the master. In any case, 'rank' wasn't of any particular importance to me; it was something for army people to worry about, or officials, not seekers-after-truth.

Every character has its own peculiarities. Gerald, no doubt about it, was a great and strong person. His self-discipline was beyond reproach: even if he was running a temperature he would arrive in the morning, or at night, park his motorcycle near the gate and visit the master, trembling with physical misery. He worked during the day as a translator for some large commercial company where he did long hours. He had a sense of humour and his soul, mind or whatever, seemed to have been dipped in the wisdom of relativity. 'Nothing is important enough to get upset about'; 'a well-organised man is comfortable, even in hell'; 'whatever is irritating will pass, in time'—I often heard him recite these truths of the east, and in his daily behaviour there were clear signs of detachment. Even so, he couldn't accept it when, on the very first morning, the head monk told him to sit at the end of the queue and, when Gerald didn't obey, took him by the shoulder and led him to the indicated spot. I heard him grumble and curse, and even a year later his protest could still be noticed. He felt hurt and humiliated.

So did I, but for a different reason. A new pain began to bother me, a pain which increased in intensity and which attacked me especially when I visited the lavatory; a burning swollen feeling. By careful groping I found a swelling, about the size of a pigeon's egg. Gerald wasn't in the monastery that day and I didn't have sufficient command of Japanese to explain to the head monk what ailed me. I asked permission to use the telephone, an old-fashioned set which was hung on a dark wall in the porch of the temple. Peter was at home, and I told him about my painful discovery.

'A pigeon's egg?' Peter asked.

I gave more details and he began to laugh.

'A pigeon's egg, ha ha. What an extraordinary association. That's a haemorrhoid; they are caused by meditation and going to the toilet in a hurry because you don't like flies and stench. The veins near your anus are bleeding and probably inflamed.'

'Yes,' I said irritably. 'And what does one do about it?'

'Nothing,' said Peter. 'Wait till I come. I'll bring you some pills and ointment and if it doesn't disappear you'll have to see the doctor. Perhaps you need an operation, which would be painful, but probably it won't be necessary. Nearly all the monks suffer from haemorrhoids and nobody has ever been to hospital. A pigeon's egg! Ha ha. The idea!'

Peter thought my idea so funny that he told everybody about it. The monks grinned when they saw me and held, without ever getting tired of the joke, an imaginary pigeon's egg between the thumb and index-finger. The head monk slapped me on the back and roared with pleasure, and the master smiled at me cheerfully when he saw me busy in the garden. I went to see the wooden statue of the Zen master in the main temple and presented my complaint.

'Why should I get idiotic, distasteful diseases when I start looking for the truth? Why don't you help me instead of allowing me being plagued by sagging veins? I am seeking final mystery, the most beautiful and glorious goal a man can aim at, so why should I be rewarded with haemorrhoids?'

The statue didn't say anything but it represented a man, a man like me, who had also looked for truth once. Perhaps he had pimples or the itch when he lived under the bridge, among beggars. I felt comforted. At least the statue hadn't laughed.

Eight

The first *sesshin* and the whale's penis

Not knowing what to expect I didn't worry much about joining the first *sesshin*. Gerald, who did know what to expect, told me it would be quite easy. 'Just a little more meditation than we usually do.' He advised me to stockpile some food, for the gate would be closed and the way to my restaurant cut off.

'Food?' I asked. 'What sort of food? Tins? But I can't very well cook my own food in the kitchen. And I am not allowed to have a hotplate in my room because the head monk says that the wires are too weak—and then there is a fire-risk of course, what with all this timber and paper and the straw mats on the floor.'

'No,' Gerald said, 'you'll have to buy some chocolate slabs and a supply of ship's biscuits. I'll get them for you.'

He also brought me a large bag of peanuts mixed with raisins, supposed to be the ideal power-food for mountaineers and meditators. Meditation is heavy work, for concentration and self-control consume a lot of energy. According to Gerald the monks' diet was no good at all. Rice gruel and radishes, sometimes noodles with soy-sauce, cucumber now and then, all eaten at speed—very unhealthy. 'They all have stomach complaints,' he said. 'Go and have a look in their rooms; there is a pot of pills on every shelf. You have to eat well, eggs and milk and bread and cheese and steak and good strong soup and a lot of fruit and fresh vegetables.'

'But Buddhists aren't allowed to kill? And they shouldn't eat meat, because that means killing indirectly.'

Gerald didn't think so. 'Nonsense. If you eat vegetables you also kill living beings. Every move you make is deadly for some insect or other. Your body kills microbes. And what is death?

An illusion, a change, a birth, a process of passing from one stage to another.'

'But why don't the monks eat meat then?'

'They do eat meat,' Gerald said, 'but not here, not in the monastery. They are often invited by people in the neighbourhood and then they eat everything which is offered to them, meat, fish, shrimps, you name it, they eat it. And because they know that the monastic fare is scanty they eat too much at such occasions. You watch them when they come back—they are all puffed up and swollen and can only just reach their rooms. Very bad for their health.'

'But why does the monastery have unhealthy rules? It is directed by enlightened spirits isn't it?'

Gerald gave me a surprised look. 'You talk like an old lady, searching for the higher life. Enlightened spirits! You mean, perhaps, that the master and the head monk know what it is all about. They do know, but they are Japanese. Japan is a country of tradition. Here they want to keep everything. Just walk into a shop and see how beautifully and carefully everything is packed. Look into the houses: everyone has his cupboards filled with ornamental boxes, every box contains another box and then there are strings to be undone and pieces of cloth to be unwrapped and then, finally, you find what they have been keeping.'

'Packing is very important here, and the training which we are following is packed with tradition. A thousand years ago some Zen monk started eating piping hot rice gruel and that's why they still do it now. And a thousand years ago an Orthodox Buddhist decided that one shouldn't eat meat and that's why Zen monks still refuse to eat meat, provided they have the feeling that someone is supervising them.'

'And sex?'

'Well,' Gerald said. 'Here in the monastery we have no girls, so it can't be done. I suppose some of the monks may have homosexual relations—it's much more accepted here than in the West anyway. But with the training and the continuous discipline, there isn't much time or opportunity for sex. You'll have to go out for it and I don't think they allow you to go out and look for it.'

'And you?'

'When I run into it I won't shy away,' Gerald said and smiled contently. 'But I haven't got much time to look for it either. During the day I work, in the evenings I have to meditate and I have to sleep a few hours too. The master expects me every morning, I have to organise my daily routine and I keep strange hours. There's no money for the whores. No, I have to wait till it comes my way; it has happened, and it will come again. I am always prepared for it.'

The day after that conversation the *sesshin* started and Gerald moved into the room next to mine, carrying a seaman's bag full of clothes and food. After the morning's meditation he furnished his room by spreading his sleeping bag on the floor. Then we were both put to work. We had to pull up weeds in the rock garden, a finicky job, because the weeds weren't much bigger than the small moss plants and were about the same colour. The monks squatted down while they worked, with their feet flat on the ground. Gerald had no trouble squatting on his haunches, but I couldn't do it easily. The head monk had often advised me to squat as much as possible, even if it hurt me. It would be good exercise, he said, and would lengthen the muscles of my thighs and loosen up my body. Eventually it would enable me to sit in the full lotus position without any pain whatever. I hadn't wanted to listen to him and had found a small wooden box which I always carried with me when I had to work in the garden and on which I could sit comfortably. This time too I had my box and was sitting on it quietly while I pulled the little weeds and talked to Gerald when the box was suddenly, and with force, kicked from under me. I toppled over backwards but jumped up, ready to attack whoever had delivered the kick. Rage is an emotion which comes very quickly and I didn't need more than one or two seconds to change from a peaceful soul into a raging maniac. I saw the head monk standing in front of me, imperturbable as usual but with a fierce light in his widely opened eyes. He had placed his legs a little apart, with his belly slightly pressed forward: the balance-position of a judoka. If I had attacked him, as I intended to, I wouldn't have been able to throw him, and if

I had wanted to kick or hit him he could have avoided me and easily have thrown me with my own power.

His calm helped me to control myself but my breathing was out of order for the next few minutes. Gerald continued working as if nothing had happened, and the head monk stooped down and took my box under his arm. I bowed, and he nodded and walked away.

'That was very nice,' Gerald said. 'In normal life a superior usually really loses his temper when he thinks that an inferior is behaving stupidly, or conceitedly if you like. And he becomes angry because he isn't quite sure of himself, or because he thinks he is important, or because he identifies himself with some "cause", like "the company" or "the job". All these causes don't, in reality, exist. It's only a matter of awareness, of knowing what you are doing. If you are pulling weeds from the moss you should do it as well as possible, without sitting down comfortably.'

'So that *is* important?' I said.

'Of course,' Gerald said. 'Nothing matters, nothing is important, but it does matter and it is important to do whatever you are doing as well as possible. Just for the hell of it. As an exercise. No more. It's like the four truths of Buddhism. Life is suffering. Suffering is caused by desire. Desire can be broken. It can be broken by walking the eightfold path. But how do you get to and on the eightfold path? By desiring to be free. By desiring to break desire. *That* desire is allright. To want to is wrong, but to want to stop wanting, well, that's excellent. Simple, really.'

'I thought Zen knows no words.'

'Yes,' Gerald said. 'And I am using a lot of words. But what I am saying isn't Zen. I have no idea what Zen is, all I have is the idea that I will know one day and that's why I am here.'

A little later the meditation started again: four periods, two hours altogether. I wanted to smoke but there was no time, and I took a few quick pulls in the lavatory and kept the rest of my cigarette in my breast pocket. At the end of the week I had a pocket full of half-smoked cigarettes, because I kept on lighting cigarettes without noticing it. In the afternoon we meditated for another two hours, and another four and a half in the evening. It seemed as if time was lengthened artificially. Because I was in pain continuously I was forced to feel the torture consciously, minute after minute. The head monk allowed me to walk sometimes, and would wave me off my seat and into the garden for a period. Time would go quickly then. Sometimes, but very rarely, he sent me to my room and I could flop down on the floor and lie on my back for twenty-five minutes. Because I fell asleep now and then, in spite of my efforts to concentrate on the *koan*, time would suddenly rush away.

It isn't possible to think about two subjects at the same time and I used this fact so as not to feel the pain. I remembered the most exciting times of my life and tried to live again through pieces of my past. That I couldn't think of the *koan* then didn't matter, I was only concerned with getting rid of the pain because I was certain that the muscles of my legs were being torn apart and the bones were being chiselled out of my feet. Again and again I imagined being back in Cape Town, coming out of the front door of my cottage, and starting my motorcycle. I recaptured every movement, I saw the trees again on the other side of the road and smelled the fragrance of the flowers in the garden. I heard the gurgling of the engine and rode off, through the narrow streets of Wynberg, towards the Waal Drive, then past the mountains and along the seashore. Sometimes I could fill an entire period of twenty-five minutes that way and Gerald congratulated me. He sat next to me and had noticed that I hadn't moved once during a whole period, apparently deep in concentration. I told him what I had been doing and he laughed.

'I do that too sometimes,' he said. 'But then I think of women I have been to bed with. The only trouble is that I become excited and it is tiring to sit with an erection for any length of time. It's much safer to ride a motorcycle.'

After the third day I began to be disturbed. The pain of sitting and the stress caused by the visits to the master began to have effect. The master had changed himself for this week into a raging lion. In his room I felt the power which came out of him,

64

and his will which forced itself on me. I *had to* give an answer to the *koan*, a satisfactory answer to a question which could not be understood, determined or analysed. I had already given every answer I could think of and none of them were any good. I wasn't even anywhere near it, he kept on saying. The beginning of any real understanding hadn't even come, I was miles, light-years, away from any indication of the truth. I was convinced he was quite right. But if I said nothing he wouldn't accept it either. I came into his room, bowed, stretched myself out on his floor three times, came back into kneeling a position, recited my *koan* and the master looked at me and said: 'Well?'

'Well nothing. Well no idea at all.'

But I didn't have to say that. I didn't know. It should be clear that I didn't know.

Sometimes he sent me back without saying anything, some-times he said a few words, and once he spoke to me for at least ten minutes. When I left his room there were tears of frustration in my eyes. I hadn't understood what he had been saying, I had too little Japanese. I had travelled through half the world to find a teacher, I had found a teacher, and I didn't understand what he was saying.

But the others had their problems, too. The head monk sat like a feared and powerful demon in the hall and shouted when he saw that we were falling asleep or dreaming off. He made us patrol regularly, and each of us in turn had to walk around with a long flat lath on the shoulder, moving slowly, dragging our feet in a threatening manner and looking at the others one by one. Whoever wobbled or was asleep was first touched on the shoulder. Then we bowed: the monk who was about to hit bowed because he was grateful that he was allowed to administer punishment, and the monk about to be hit was also grateful. Then we hit eight times. The monk who was beaten had to lean forward so that he could be hit on the muscles of the back. We hit quickly, allowing the lath to spring back so that it could only make contact for a split second. I had to learn the trick first, on a monk who had tied a cushion on his back. The lath, when it isn't handled properly, can inflict real damage, especially when it hits the spine. The monks in the hall often wore padded waistcoats; I wore an extra jersey. Even so the pain was sharp, and at the end of the week I had a blue cross on my back. But this pain couldn't be compared with the pain in my legs. When I was hit the pain would disappear very quickly but the pain in my legs never seemed to pass—even when I walked the torture continued. The monks showed their sympathy and enquired regularly how I was getting on. That helped. A young monk who had hurt his leg while chopping wood was in almost continuous pain, too, as his wound wouldn't heal properly. I saw him cry when it was my turn to go round with the stick and when I passed him without appearing to notice that he was moving about and obviously not meditating, the head monk shouted and I was forced to go back and give him his eight whacks. He bowed politely and smiled when I met him later that day in the dining room.

I began to mumble to myself and walked into walls and trees. When I said something the words weren't connected and my sentences had neither beginning nor end. Gerald was also showing signs of abnormality.

When we were cleaning the lavatories together and I had to control myself so as not to vomit, he suddenly started a story about whales.

'A whale has a penis as long as a full grown man, did you know that?'

I said that I had never thought about whales' penises but Gerald didn't hear me.

'Yes,' he said. 'Very big, unbelievably big. I have seen grey whales copulating, just off the coast of California. They jumped clear out of the water and fell back with a splash. You can hear a splash like that miles away. It's really something.'

When I looked at him his eyes weren't focusing and he looked clean through me. The surroundings in which I lived began to irritate me. I was looking for a seat, a chair, a bench, anything I could sit or lie on. But there was nothing of that kind about. Empty rooms everywhere, with straw mats on the floor, and nothing but a few uncomfortable rocks and gravestones in the garden. I couldn't lie down on the ground either: it had been raining a lot and the ground was wet through. My room was prohibited territory. I was allowed to sleep in it from 11 p.m. to 3 a.m., but for the rest of the day I couldn't use it unless the head monk sent me there to lie down for half an hour and that didn't happen every day.

Gerald thought that I was living a luxurious life. He asked me whether I was meditating in the garden.

'In the garden? What do I have to do in the garden? We meditate in the meditation hall don't we?'

'Yes,' Gerald said. 'But you are expected to meditate for an extra half hour in the garden every night. Just go into the garden at eleven o'clock at night tonight. You'll find us all there; we sit on the rocks and on the gravestones—everybody has his own place. Half an hour free meditation, that's compulsory.'

I didn't believe him, and took a few minutes off my cherished sleeping time that night to see for myself. He was right. But I didn't feel any compulsion to follow the good example. I thought I was doing enough, more than enough. I would start meditating in the garden only if they dragged me out there by my hair, and that night I dug myself into my sleeping-bag, grunted with pleasure and dropped far away before I had even managed to touch the bottom of the bag with my toes.

Nine

A little black magic

Every morning the master made the rounds of the temple and we, the monks and I, followed him through the long corridors of the monastery. At every niche he stopped, and we stopped too, of course, and recited a prayer, mumbling and slurring the words, for our own benefit or whoever was represented in the niche. Sometimes there were statues of Bodhisatva's, sometimes a Buddha was shown, in meditation, or while lecturing, but there were also Chinese or Japanese gods who had no relation to Buddhism at all. There was even a fat little God of physical well-being. Flowers were placed in vases and the master lit incense sticks. During one of these performances I remembered that my passport had to be renewed. This meant I would have to go to Kobe. Have to, because the authority of worldly power, in this case that of the queen of the Netherlands, could not be ignored by the monks.

The head monk, for this reason, allowed me to break my promised eight months' continuous stay in the monastery and gave me an entire day off, and I took the tram to the station. I had put on a new nylon shirt which wouldn't let perspiration through and it was a warm day. I looked at freedom through the open windows of the bumping and shaking tram and realised that I had lived for almost five months in seclusion. I had been through the gate every now and then but never further than, at the most, half a mile. I saw crowds of people, enormous advertisements for films, showing half-naked women and aggressive men handling firearms, show-windows full of puppets dressed in new clothes, and grey heavy buildings housing banks and trading companies. I felt relieved but also irritated. I hadn't chosen the monastic life but rather had accepted it, as a means to an end, but now that I was free of the pressure of the monastery, I longed for the silence of the garden with its lovely grey and green shades and the monotonous robes of the monks. Here there was too much bustle; it was too full, too exaggerated. The screaming colours of the advertisements weren't necessary, the shouting and laughing were annoying. Perhaps it would be a good idea to force everybody to meditate regularly, in halls which would be built in all the cities of the world. Every evening from seven to nine, compulsory silence, and every morning at 3.30, an unavoidable visit to a master. A master to every street.

And nature would have to be restored so that all cities would be surrounded by vast forests, and in the forests huts could be built for hermits who didn't feel the need to work under a master. A public soup-kitchen in every forest. And as a means of transport we could use the horse again, or the camel, perhaps elephants as well so that we would all learn to live with animals again, with beings of another order. And meanwhile technology could continue, with efficient factories holding monopolies and producing the best quality which scientists could develop, and fast noiseless trains and ships and aeroplanes and rockets so that everybody could have his food and drink and clothes and other necessities with a minimum outlay of energy. The tram bounced along and I reached the station. There were a lot of people about and because I didn't want to push my way through them I almost missed my train. There was plenty of room to move about but Japanese always seem to push each other on platforms; at first they wait calmly and behave in a civilised manner, but when the train appears they are suddenly caught up in a fierce panic and everyone has to get through the door at the same time. That I didn't want to push with the others seemed, to my mind, proof of having gained a little by the monastic discipline. I had, obviously, become calm and selfless. But I had to admit that I had never pushed, not in Rotterdam either when the trams were full. I had preferred, in those days, to walk to school or to wait for the next tram. The need to find out whether the training was having any effect had long been an obsession, as if *satori*, enlightenment, reaching the holy goal, were bound to a certain place and I should be getting closer and closer to that particular spot. 'Have I got anywhere or not? Am I getting more detached from whatever is happening around me? Am I understanding more? Am I getting lighter, more loose?' I kept on asking myself, although the master often warned me against the folly of such measuring.

'You'll find out anyway,' he would say, 'you shouldn't worry like that. Your achievements are quite unimportant; rather try to solve your *koan*. What is the answer to your *koan*? What do you have to tell me? Say it!'

But I said nothing and continued counting non-existent milestones.

In the train I found myself pressed against several people, one of them a woman, some twenty years old perhaps. I had already looked at her and noticed that she was beautiful, with rather a sensuous body, large slanting eyes and thick black hair. Attracting the attention of women I don't know has always been below my sense of dignity, or perhaps I am too shy for that sort of thing; anyway I didn't try it that time either, although I was enjoying the contact with her body. I thought of the concentration exercise I had been doing for months. It could be tried. Before I knew it I began to breathe deeply and very slowly and fixed the image of the woman, as I remembered it from one short glance, in my thoughts. I tried to think of nothing else and when I knew that I had gained a certain measure of concentration I ordered her to press herself against me. And miracle of miracles, she obeyed. I felt how she rubbed herself, softly and furtively at first, but gradually more firmly, against me and I heard her breathing becoming deep and heavy. And while she rubbed herself against the side of my body she trembled.

'What now?' I thought, for the contact made my blood surge. 'Shall I talk to her? Shall I ask her to get off at the next station? We can go to a hotel room—I have enough money on me. And I can go to Kobe this afternoon. The consul has time to spare.'

But my excitement broke my concentration, the woman was released and moved away a little. She looked up at me and I saw a troubled look in her eyes. The train happened to pull up at a station and she got out. My skin was prickly under the nylon shirt and sweat was running down my face. 'Black magic isn't all it's cracked up to be,' I thought. 'A lot of trouble and waste of energy. Suppose she had gone with me, so what? An adventure, a step into a vacuum, a memory to disturb future meditation. One shouldn't shy away from it, Gerald said. Maybe he went in for tricks in trains as well?' I asked him later, but he pretended not to know what I was talking about.

I didn't tell the master. The experiment seemed clear enough and I could do without his sarcastic wit. That someone who has trained his will can influence others, without saying anything, without doing anything observable, had now been proved. The monks told me that there are witches in Japan who, for a certain fee, are prepared to perform tricks. A troublesome competitor or a rival in love can be forced to break his leg or catch a nasty cold, depending on the price and on the concentration of the witch. 'But,' the monks said 'you have to be very careful; the power which is caused by concentration continues to exist and will in the end turn itself against whoever created it. Witches punish themselves, and their clients pay a heavy price in the end.'

I comforted myself by the idea that I hadn't wanted anything evil, just some sexual pleasure, shared cosiness with a climax and no harm done.

In Kobe I faced a heavy, colourless, concrete building, and admired the lion of the Netherlands, growling and snarling on a colourful gilded sign above the entrance. Somewhere in this building a representative of the Fatherland sat behind a large desk, and the little black book in my back-pocket proved my membership of this club. Not that they would do anything for me, except ask for money in exchange for a rubber stamp; it said so in the little black book. I couldn't expect anything, couldn't count on anything, except the right to be recognised as a fellow countryman. And that is what they did, although they did go further. I was given a cup of good coffee and a Dutch cigar and was allowed to sit in a heavy leather armchair.

'You are staying in a Buddhist monastery,' the chancellor

said. 'We heard about you. There's someone in Kobe who would like to be introduced to you. If you agree I'll phone him; perhaps you would like to meet him.'

I agreed. I had nothing further to do and although the monastery gate would be closed at 9 p.m. as it was every evening, I knew that I would be able to get in through the side entrance, by lifting a small secret lever. The head monk had promised not to close the side entrance that night. I could stay out till 3 a.m. the next morning.

The chancellor telephoned and within ten minutes a gentleman by the name of Leo Marks presented himself and greeted me enthusiastically. He thanked the public servant for his co-operation and invited me to lunch. In his car, an oversized Chrysler, black and either brand new or very well kept, I had the opportunity to study him. A tall man, in his early forties, greying at the temples and obviously homosexual. I was quite sure of this although I didn't have any proof. A lot of men wear old-rose coloured ties, and the whiff of perfume could be everyday aftershave.

'I don't suppose you want Japanese food,' he said. 'You must have enough of that in the monastery. What would you like to eat?'

The Chrysler looked expensive enough, so I didn't have to be modest.

'Real turtle soup,' I said, 'with a drop of sherry in it. And a large underdone steak with salads on the side, and something with whipped cream to finish it off. And coffee. And a cigar.'

'It's a good sign when a man knows what he wants,' Mr Marks said, and parked his car with some difficulty. 'This car is far too large but I need her. I work for a company which deals in large objects. We sell ships and complete installations for factories and we deal in expensive art sometimes. In our game one has to make an impression. Solid. A lot of ready cash behind one.'

As I would learn later, he was, in spite of the glamour which surrounded him, a pleasant and modest man. At table, in a small Japanese restaurant where the western style was imitated to perfection, so perfect that the result seemed better than the example used, he told me about his interest in Zen and Japanese art. He had started, years ago, a collection of Japanese woodblock prints. Anything which he considered to be a prize item in his collection turned out to be inspired by Zen and he had begun to study this form of Buddhism. He had been living in Japan for a long time and spoke the language reasonably well. He had visited Zen priests but had never risked a meeting with a Zen master.

'It would be going too far' he said, when I got to know him better. 'I don't want to expose myself. *Koan*-study seems to be real torture. It isn't that I can't detach myself from my possessions or my way of life, or the expensive impression I make on others, but I don't want to give up my own idea of what I am. If one solves a *koan* one commits, to my way of thinking anyway, suicide. Not by putting a bullet into one's skull or by poisoning one's stomach or blood, that way you only destroy your body. All of us think that we will continue after death, in some spiritual body or something to that effect. A Christian goes to heaven, a Buddhist starts a next life. Even an atheist doesn't really believe that he will be obliterated altogether, he hasn't got the courage to think himself into such absolute negativity.'

'And meditation?' I asked. 'Have you ever considered meditating? Did you ever try?'

'No, of course not. I have tried but I can't fold up my legs. And why should I be able to fold up my legs? I am a westerner; we should be able to follow other possibilities in the way of training.'

'Like what?' I asked, but he didn't answer. I didn't insist. A good Buddhist, according to the books I had read, is no missionary, but tolerates the thoughts, decisions, way of life, of others. Toleration leads to friendship. Friendship always wins. There has never been a Buddhist war.

Leo Marks became a haven to me in Japan. When the *sesshins* were over and the discipline in the monastery relaxed a little I was allowed to spend an occassional weekend in Kobe, and the Chrysler, handled by an impeccable driver, would meet me at the station and whisk me to Leo's house where I could do whatever I wanted to do. I read on his balcony overlooking the sea, sank deeply into a well-upholstered cane chair, and rested my feet on the balcony railing. I smoked cigars, watched the fishing boats setting out at dawn, ate solid Dutch meals and drank jenever. His Japanese paid friends, graceful in their kimonos, didn't disturb me. He never introduced them to me and I smiled at them when I happened to meet them in the large three-storied mansion. I selected books from his library, and read for the first time the work of van Gulik, the Dutch ambassador and sinologue who wrote thrillers about ancient China and the famous magistrate Dee. Judge Dee thinks along strict Confucian lines and believes firmly in morality but when confronted with real Buddhist and Taoist masters, who make fun of him, respects them because Dee himself is a man of genius, with an incorruptible and sincere mind, capable of realising the depth of their teaching.

During one of these weekends I found myself at a party, a party run according to the rules of what is known as fashionable society. For the first time in my life I wore evening clothes, borrowed from Leo. If I didn't move about too much the suit seemed to fit me. The ladies of the party showed a lot of interest in me. It was a curious sensation to feel that I, the floor-scrubber and weed-puller of the monastery, was a mysterious man in this environment, romantic, a mystic. With a cigar in my mouth and a glass filled with whisky and tinkling icecubes in my hand, as rigid as an officer of the Dutch *marechaussee* (if I bent over I ran the risk of my trousers falling down, I had to press out my stomach to keep them up), I deigned to come down to the level of these ladies of the world and admired their breasts, gracefully pressed up by invisible structures of plastic, while a jazz combo deepened the atmosphere. I didn't mind the part, but it became a little ludicrous after a while. The master would have grinned if he had been able to see me. 'And the *koan*?' The ladies wanted to know about the *koan*, too. 'Now what, really, is a *koan* supposed to be? How does one explain the sound of *one* clapping hand?' A book had just come out which listed a number of *koans* and Zen anecdotes and everybody in the company had read it. 'Is it really true that a Zen master broke his pupil's leg by slamming the gate on him? Do they use harsh methods like that to cause insight? Is it true that a Chinese disciple cut off his own arm to prove to his master that he was really interested in Zen?' 'I suppose so,' I said. But my master never broke anybody's leg and he had never given me the impression that he expected me to maim myself. It wouldn't be a bad idea, I thought. If I could be quite sure that an amputated limb would automatically cause insight, the method might be preferable to the endless torture on the meditation bench.

I was also asked several times if I had been given a *koan*, and if so, if I had solved that *koan*. A gentleman introduced himself as a graduate in Zen Buddhism. He had, he said, taken a course at Leiden university. 'I know the sound of *one* clapping hand', he whispered into my ear and looked at me as if we both belonged to a secret brotherhood. 'I don't,' I said. 'Yes, yes,' he said roguishly, 'real insight is never displayed openly.'

I drank too much that evening but I don't think anybody noticed. Leo took me, when the party was over, to a brothel where the inmates were boys, some of them dressed as girls. Homosexuality and transvestism were prohibited by law at that time, if linked with prostitution, and the brothel-keeper kept a few real girls at the bar to keep up appearances. It was a rare phenomenon for a man who liked girls to come into the establishment, and when the girls discovered that I spoke Japanese, albeit badly, their joy knew no bounds. I was fondled and fussed over and Leo gave me a fatherly look, and had me fetched in the morning by taxi. He had gone home to think about Buddhism. 'I am a Buddhist of course,' he said 'but if I reflect a little it may be that I shall gain enough courage to practice my faith.' I wished him strength with a wave of my cigar. 'I admire you,' he said, and bowed down over me, correct and courteous as always. 'What you are doing I have always wanted to do. That's why I am glad that I met you.'

'Yes,' I said, 'look where you have brought me.'

'You wanted to come yourself,' Leo said, 'and it has got nothing to do with it. The little dog has the Buddha nature, and these whores too.'

'Happy Easter,' I said. My frivolity irritated him but the next day he was as kind and friendly as ever.

Ten

Rohatsu, week of weeks

Sesshins, the meditation weeks of a Zen monastery, fill the first seven days of six months of the year. A week has seven days; I had forgotten that fact. I was still thinking that a week had five days of regularly repeated obligations, followed by two days of another order altogether, two days in which to forget the five days.

But a week in a Zen monastery has seven days and not one minute is given away. Every meditation period lasts exactly twenty-five minutes, and the pause between two periods lasts five minutes. At eleven p.m. the last stroke on the large copper bell ebbs away slowly and only then is there sleep. Some *sesshins* contain more meditation hours that others: in summer, when there is a lot of work in the ornamental and vegetable gardens, seven to nine hours a day; in winter eleven hours a day.

But it could be much worse, as I heard from the monks, although I didn't believe them at first. The first week of December is Rohatsu. Rohatsu is the *sesshin* which rules all *sesshins*. Fifteen hours of meditation per day: from 2 a.m. to 4 a.m., from 5 a.m. to 11 a.m.; from 1 p.m. to 5 p.m.; from 7 p.m. to midnight. That is seventeen hours altogether, but the visits to the master take time and are deducted from the meditation time.

I couldn't believe it. It had to be an impossible exercise, even if there were regular beating up and shouting. No human being can sit still for fifteen hours a day, and under stress as well, with an unanswerable question tucked away in his belly. I would faint or go raving mad. Certainly, Buddha had meditated for weeks on end, under a tree, on a rock. But that was 2500 years ago. A holy man, shrouded in the haze of antiquity. Christ had meditated in the desert for forty days on end. That was 2000 years ago. But I was a westerner of today—a restless, nervous, noisy seeker without insight, without power. With some sense of humour and a somewhat indifferent outlook on daily life one cannot sit still for fifteen hours a day. All right, I had managed to sit still for eleven hours a day, but with a lot of wobbling about and secret glances at others and at my watch, and with rest periods of an hour or more so that I could sleep or sit on a gravestone and smoke cigarettes and dream.

I tried not to think about this coming horror, just as in the past I had pushed away the image of an approaching visit to the dentist or an examination, drawing nearer and nearer. But this was something quite different. Dentists and examiners had been pushed on me by strong powers around me, powers outside myself, grim and overbearing powers against which I couldn't defend myself. But what had forced me to undergo a training which asked me to perform an absolutely impossible feat?

I sat on the little staircase leading down into the garden from my room, smoked and looked about and saw the ornamental fir trees, cut and guided into enchanting shapes, now lightly covered by a thin layer of snow: a miraculous and beautiful view. I had said something about it to the head monk who happened to pass by and he had stopped for a moment, looked politely at the indicated trees, and had admitted drily that they were beautiful. 'Just like a picture!'

His remark annoyed me. 'Just like a picture.' What an inane thing to say. Limited, bourgeois. And this was supposed to be an enlightened man in whom *satori*, the lightning of sudden real insight, should have taken place at least several times, for he had finished his *koan* study.

A Zen *koan* exists which asks why Bodhidharma, the first Zen master, went to China: a symbolic question, an essential question, a question in the order of 'What is the essence of Buddhism?' The answer which one Zen master accepted was: 'The fir tree in the temple garden.' Just a tree, like the tree standing here in front of me. Because a tree shows the perfect beauty in which

77

everything else is expressed, and especially the essence of Buddhism and the reason of Bodhidharma's long wanderings through a strange country. I could feel that quite well. In any case, I liked trees. But if I were to say to the master that the truth of everything, the purpose of life, is expressed in a tree, he would pick up his bell and ring me out of the room or he would grunt and shake his head.

And that was why I had come, to visit an old Japanese gentleman who ridiculed everything I said or could say, and to sit still for fifteen hours a day on a mat, for seven days on end, while the monks whacked me on the back with a four-foot long lath made of strong wood.

I cursed softly. What on earth was wrong with me? Why couldn't I live normally and do my best, like my brothers and sisters, like my father had always done? My grandmother, whom I never knew, would have said that one musn't break one's head about questions which cannot be answered. My mother had asked her what exists outside the universe. 'If you come to the end of the universe,' my grandmother said, 'You will see that everything has been pasted over with newspapers.' An intelligent answer, which had satisfied my mother. Why couldn't I be content with an endless wall, built of wooden lathe-work and pasted over with the *New Rotterdam Herald*?

But while I mumbled to myself, and lit my fourth cigarette that morning, Rohatsu was coming closer and I knew that I wouldn't run away from it. Han-san and Ka-san, and whatever the other sans might be called, the young monks would all have to get through it.

Country lads, given by their fathers to the monastery. If they could do it, couldn't I do it? I can't do it, I thought. These country lads were Japanese, easterners, quiet and patient boys with a large reserve of inherited tolerance. And I knew that some of them had already solved *koans*. Perhaps Japanese are privileged beings who have a special talent for attaining insight into the mysteries.

Perhaps I'll be able to do it next year, I thought. If I train myself for another year I shall be able to sit comfortably in half-lotus. I'll ask for dispensation; the head monk will surely realise that I can't get through this week of terror. He may be tough and severe but for me, a westerner with exceptionally stiff legs, he will make an exception. I cursed again for I remembered that I had called him, a few days ago, to the meditation hall to show him that I was sitting much better. My thigh muscles had grown a little for I could, with a little extra exertion, get my right foot on the instep of my left foot, and if I pushed and strained and pulled, even on the calf of my left leg. With an extra pillow under my bottom I could gain a reasonable balance. He had smiled and patted me on the shoulder. Why couldn't I have restrained myself, why did I always have to show off and endeavour to show any so-called progress to the world?

That day I was called to see the head monk and two of his colleagues. They spoke to me at length, but I didn't understand them very well. After several repetitions I nodded. I had understood that they weren't very happy with my progress and that this Rohatsu would be a final test. If I managed to get through the week all right I could stay in the monastery, and the master would continue to receive me. But if I gave up halfway through Rohatsu I should have to leave the monastery. They even gave me the name of a small hotel in the neighbourhood where I could go and stay.

I bowed and returned to my room. Very well. What has to be done has to be done. I swore that I would get through the week even if my legs were so stiffened with cramp that they would never be usable again, and even if my mind gave way. Even if I went insane I would sit it out, if need be as an idiot, dribbling at the mouth, but I wouldn't enable them to chase me out of the monastery. I had another two days to prepare myself. I bought chocolate slabs and ordered a large bag of the peanut and raisin mixture via Gerald. I bought an extra heavy jersey and six undershirts; I would wear three at a time so as to keep the stick off my skin. I even bought the heating apparatus which most of the monks were using. It looked like a spectacle case but instead of spectacles contained smouldering sticks of charcoal. A monk had told me that these cases, if worn next to the stomach, gave a splendid heat which spread right through the body. The stomach is nearest the plexus solaris, the most important nerve knot of the human body. Once it gets warm everything becomes warm. I had heard a lot about the plexus solaris. The master always pointed to his belly. That's where the real feeling is, the real centre of observation. Music shouldn't be listened to but felt, here in your belly. Other people should be felt. The *koan* should be tucked into the belly. Don't think with your brain but concentrate here, in your belly.

During the meditation exercises I had learned to regulate my breathing: first take a short breath, then press out the belly and 'push the breath into the belly', and then keep it there. The master was quite a small man but he had such strength in his belly muscles that he could push my fist, and the weight of my body behind it, back by merely extending his stomach.

When Rohatsu began the head monk locked my room. During that week we wouldn't just meditate in the hall but sleep there as well, if sleep it could be called, for we were only given two hours a day, from midnight to 2 a.m. I came into the hall with my sleeping bag under my arm. A small cupboard would hold my chocolate, nuts and raisins, toothbrush, soap and small towel. The clothes I was wearing would have to last all week. I sat down, moved into the most comfortable position I could find and the head monk struck his bell. Two o'clock in the morning. I had all my jerseys on and my three undershirts. The spectacle-case glowed away, wrapped in a thin piece of cloth, against my stomach. It was freezing in the meditation hall but I didn't feel the cold. The first period of the first day. I would count them all carefully, one by one.

The head monk delivered a small lecture.

'This is going to be heavy going. Use this week well. Think of nothing, become one with your *koan*. Forget your friends, forget the meditation hall, forget yourself, forget time. Don't think of your body. Don't think of food or cigarettes or sleep.'

And don't move. The young monks shouldn't move either. Neither should the newcomers move. Nor the westerners. There were only two westerners, Gerald and myself, and Gerald never moved. I did, but I wouldn't be able to do it now. He had meant me and he would pay special attention to me, and shout: 'Jan-san, sit still. You are disturbing the others.' I didn't want him to shout at me. I wanted to draw attention to myself because I was doing something well, not because I was always doing everything the wrong way. Not to be able to do things well was getting a bit of a bore.

The head monk was also becoming a bit of a bore lately. I would show him that I could handle him for a change, that he didn't have to pour his will all over me all the time.

And when the spectacle-case became too hot for comfort I didn't move.

My belly was getting strangely warm. I didn't understand it, couldn't I manage this either? All the monks had these cases and I saw them sitting all around me, apparently at peace and quietly happy in their concentration. Why did I have this glowing belly? The feeling of warmth was slowly changing into pain. I had the unmistakable feeling that my skin was getting scorched. But I didn't move; another ten minutes and the bell would be struck. For the first time I felt no pain in my legs. It seemed as if I didn't have any legs. But I *did* have a belly, and my belly was on fire.

When the bell was struck I jumped off my seat and rushed out and pulled all my shirts out of my trousers. I had a burn of several square inches. Gerald, who came to see what ailed me this time, shook his head and looked puzzled.

'Did you just wrap the case in that thin piece of cloth?'

'Yes,' I said; 'shouldn't I have?'

'No, you shouldn't have. You should have wrapped it in a towel and then have stuck the whole bundle in a belly-wrap. You can buy them in any store.' He started to laugh but controlled himself. 'That's a nasty burn. It should be treated.'

He went back to the hall to speak to the head monk and we were both excused for the next period. The cook, the only monk who didn't take part in the meditation as he had to cook for thirty people, spread some ointment on the wound and bandaged it neatly. He tried to behave in a compassionate manner but finally broke down and began to laugh as well.

'These cases are really prohibited,' the cook said, 'just like the padded vests and waistcoats the monks wear.'

'Yes,' Gerald agreed. 'And you don't need a case at all if you concentrate properly, you can sit in the snow stark naked. You could sit in a fire as well.' He addressed the cook: 'True or not?'

'Yes,' the monk said. 'With concentration you can do anything. But you are in my way, both of you. Go back to the hall. The head monk is waiting for you.'

The first day passed. The second day passed as well. The third day wasn't too bad. The fourth day was one long interminable hell of pain and boredom and frustrated restlessness. That day I was being hit regularly and I hated the monks. I had to use all my strength to keep myself from jumping off my seat to attack them. Gerald, who wanted to say something to me during one of the short breaks, stepped back when he saw the murderous expression on my face and found another spot to lean against a wall and relax for a few minutes. The head monk snapped some command at me and I snarled and ground my teeth in response. I had to light three cigarettes one after another, the first two had become powder in my hands.

The fourth day is the worst, the others confirmed later. Six laymen from the neighbourhood had come to join us that week: a medical doctor, the local baker and four men I didn't know. During the fourth day they all disappeared. Even their cushions had gone. Their disappearance wasn't discussed by the monks. Japanese are polite, if something goes wrong; the fact is recognised and greeted in silence. But Gerald and I were rough foreigners, barbarians from the west, and we grinned at each other.

Gerald's face had become hollow, his cheekbones jutted right out, and his eyelids were red and seemed inflamed. Our hands were thick and puffy from lying in our laps, hour after hour. We stumbled as we walked. The master seemed very changed as well. For the first time I saw him in the meditation hall and he was with us continuously, except when he was away in his little house to receive us. His eyes had sunk well back into their sockets, and his shrunken face bristled with the beginning of a sparse beard and moustache. Instead of his usually gleaming skull I now saw a fringe of grey down.

But his fatigue was only on the outside; he was the same hard pusher and puller I knew from the former *sesshins*. His little room trembled with power, and more than ever before I had the feeling that I was crushing myself against a thick wall but that the wall, in some mysterious way, was trying to help me—that there was an opening, and that I could find that opening. The sixth day the pain became so bad that I began to groan and the head monk sent me out of the hall. I had to walk up and down on a slightly elevated stone-tiled path, and on both sides, some three feet below me, were low shrubs. I must have closed my eyes and suddenly I found I was lying in the brushwood, not knowing who I was or where I was. I hadn't fainted, I had fallen asleep. The head monk heard the thump of my fall, then some rustling of leaves, then nothing. He came, exceptionally, for he hadn't left the hall except for meals in the main temple, to see what was wrong, and he woke me up and pulled me back onto the path where he brushed the leaves off my clothes and hit me softly in the face.

'Wake up, it won't be long now.' In his eyes I saw warm friendship, an emotion which I hadn't recognised in his face before.

The seventh day passed reasonably quickly, I fell asleep, hit the monks, was beaten up in return, visited the master five times a day, and was marched to the dining room and taken back to the hall under escort of the head monk and Ke-san, his assistant. Nothing irritated me any more. The last day. At midnight the exercise would be over, the end was in sight, nothing worse that what I had already experienced could happen now.

I counted the minutes of the last period. Another twenty-four minutes. Another twenty-three minutes. The bell was struck. I expected a general relaxing and joy, laughter, sudden talking, but the quiet tense atmosphere in the hall did not change. I looked at Gerald who was studying his watch. I hissed at him and he shrugged his shoulders.

I went outside, washed my face with cold water and waited for the others to come out, but to my surprise the bell was struck again. The meditation continued and I was late. I ran back, bowed to the head monk to excuse myself and he pointed at my seat. When he saw that his order bewildered me he whispered that it would go on for another two hours. I was told later that he had only told *me* this; he had wanted to add another exercise by giving us the impression that he was going on for another complete day, but he probably thought that I had suffered enough and defined the duration of the added practice.

I got through the two hours, slumped in my seat and dulled into a half-sleep. The hall was not patrolled this time, and I could wobble if I wanted to. I felt no pain, only a soft buzzing in my legs, and the burn on my belly ached a little. All I had to do was fight the sleep which threatened to engulf me. I wasn't sufficiently in balance to be safe when asleep. If I toppled over I would make a spectacle of myself and might crack my skull on the stone floor below me as well. At 2 a.m. the head monk struck his bell with force, and its clear sound sang through the hall. Gi-san jumped down, rushed outside and attacked the temple drum, and the two youngest monks began to strike the six-feet high, massive bell in the clock-tower. We streamed out of the hall, after a last formal bow in the direction of the altar. I lit a cigarette and laughed at Gerald, who embraced me and mumbled something which I didn't catch. The head monk shook me by the hand.

'The bath is ready. I'll wash your back. It's tradition. The last will be the first. You jump in first.'

I saw steam rise from the bathhouse: the cook had taken care of everything, he had done all the chores by himself all week and was, if possible, even more exhausted than the others. His soft wide face was split by a tremendous smile.

My clothes were caked to my body and I didn't know how quickly I could strip them off. I kept on pouring bowls of hot water down my back and front while the head monk, naked and tiny, massaged my back with his strong hands. In a corner sat Gerald flat on the floor with his legs stretched wide apart, brushing his teeth till his beard was white with foam. The young monks splashed contentedly and talked softly to each other. The story of the case which had burned my skin was repeated many times and everybody squealed with pleasure, even the head monk, even the master who came to see how we were doing and who had put on a clean bathrobe. We spent more than an hour in the bath-house and I shaved my stubby beard hair by hair.

When the head monk told me again how pleased he was with my effort I said that I didn't understand him. Hadn't he told me that I would *have* to get through Rohatsu? That I would be sent down if I dropped out?

'What?' he asked. 'What is this nonsense?'

Gerald was asked to join in the conversation and I finally realised that I had misunderstood the instructions which the head monk and his two colleagues had given me. They had tried to explain to me that they didn't expect me to be able to get through the complete exercise. But I could, they had repeated at least three times, give up. Only, they couldn't have me wandering about the monastery while the others were trying to get through Rohatsu. That's why they had given me the name and address of a hotel close by. It took a little time before it all got through to me. Gerald explained it again.

'Never mind,' the head monk said. 'I am glad you didn't understand me. Because whatever your reasons were, you pulled through. That's very good.'

Gerald sat down and laughed till he had tears in his eyes, I had to throw cold water over him to make him shut up. 'You,' Gerald said 'are such a nitwit that you'll enter Nirvana by mistake.'

After the bathhouse the monks went to the kitchen for break-fast. I saw a wide variety of Japanese delicacies on the tables, radishes, sour plums, seaweed, small bowls with sauces. The head monk put his hand on my shoulder. 'Not for you. That's for us, we like this type of food. You and Gerald have been invited out by Peter; he is waiting for you.'

When I heard the pebbles crunch under my wooden sandals, felt the clean clothes against my skin, and inhaled the smoke of a cigarette, and knew that it was all over, that Rohatsu had faded into the past, I felt such a wave of happiness surge through me that I stopped. Gerald pushed me forward. 'Peter has made an American breakfast, mark my words.'

And so it was. There was a neatly laid out table waiting for us, with dishes full of crisp rolls, bacon and eggs, fresh butter, a large pot of coffee, and tins of marmalade and cherry jam. Peter kept on toasting rolls and pouring coffee and frying eggs till we rolled over backwards on the floormats. That day was a holiday. I slept for a few hours and then woke up. The rhythm of my existence was disturbed and I couldn't go back to sleep. I read till I became drowsy again. The rest of the day I spent sleeping, walking about the gardens, and eating. All stress had gone. The *koan* rumbled vaguely on the horizon of my consciousness but that was all. It was very quiet in my mind; the only feeling I was aware of was one of intense contentment.

Eleven

The eightfold path and a jump into the swamp

In India a hermit was meditating on the shore of a river when he was disturbed by a young man. The young man knelt down and said:

'Master, I want to become your disciple.'

'Why?' asked the master.

'Because I want to find God.'

The master jumped up, took the young man by the scruff of the neck, dragged him to the river and pushed his head under water. After a minute the master released the young man and pulled him out of the river. The young man spat out some of the water which he got in his mouth and began to cough. After a while he became quiet.

'What did you want most of all while I kept you under water?' asked the master.

'Air,' said the young man.

'Very well,' the master said. 'Go back to wherever you have come from, and come back to me when you want God as much as you wanted air just now.'

I hadn't come to the monastery to find God. I wanted to have an explanation of existence, an explanation so clear that all my questions would fall away by themselves. I wanted to know why everything had been started, because it couldn't be, I thought, that it had all been started just to finish again. Why all this trouble, this pain, this looking for something which couldn't be found? Perhaps the explanation would be identical to the idea of 'God', but that wouldn't make me a seeker after God; I would prefer to describe myself as an alarmed soul. But whatever I was, devout or alarmed, I had wanted to find something. I had come to a master who, I thought, had what I wanted to find or who at least knew the way to whatever I was looking for. He had shown me the way but I wasn't following it.

I did, during the months following Rohatsu, all sorts of things. I had found possibilities of making monastic life pleasant. When I 'meditated' I didn't even try to concentrate. I counted the minutes, estimated how long it would take to the next bell, dozed, trained my body not to fall over when I slept, and dreamed. I imagined whatever can be imagined, to get through the time. The pain bothered me much less now and I began to enjoy sitting, nicely balanced, without being troubled by my legs or back. I enjoyed the meals which I ate, on medical prescription as before, in the restaurants of the neighbourhood. It was pleasant after a good meal, to sit quietly, smoke and sip coffee. I always carried a book and would spend another half hour reading. The lessons in Japanese ,which I was still taking, were very interesting as well; and the hieroglyphics, which had once been so mysterious, now began to have meaning and I exercised diligently and filled notebook after notebook with scribbles. I could make myself understood and when the Japanese, always polite, complimented me on my progress I would glow with pride. And there was the bathhouse and the laundry-man who washed and ironed my clothes so neatly. I had even discovered a barber's-shop which employed girls and I went there regularly to be shaved and have the muscles of my neck massaged.

A book on Tibetan Buddhism told me that whoever knows how to organise his life can be comfortable anywhere, even in hell. I quite agreed. I had managed to be comfortable in a Zen monastery.

That I couldn't solve the *koan*, I accepted. *Koans* are difficult, anyone knows that. Nobody really expected me to solve the *koan* in a hurry. Hadn't there been Zen monks who had fought their *koan* for sixteen years before they broke through the wall? Well then. And although the master still gave me the impression every day that he really expected me to solve the *koan* that very day, well, that was part of his game. He had to pretend that I would bring him the answer here and now. But he knew, of course, that I wasn't anywhere near the answer.

But the *sesshins* kept on coming every month, and then my pleasures stopped and I would have to make an effort. During *sesshins* nobody could escape the pressure of the monastery; the young monks saw their roads of escape cut off and exerted themselves to accomplish the hopeless task. The head monk pushed and the master pulled and they were beaten up and shouted at and sometimes I even meditated when I didn't have to and sat in my room, or somewhere in the garden, and tried to lose my thoughts and grab the *koan* which always slipped away again.

I noticed that the young monks had discovered ways to break the rules of the monastery. They couldn't, as I did, visit restaurants and other public establishments, because they wore the monastic garb and had their heads shaved. But they did have civilian clothes, hidden in their rooms or in a corner of the temple where nobody came. When they put on a suit and a cap nobody would recognise them, and I saw them climb over the wall at night. They even had a special little ladder for that purpose.

'Whatever do you do when you are over the wall?' I asked Han-san, the youngest monk, who had become my friend.

'As long as you don't tell anyone,' Han-san said. 'We go to the cinema, and sometimes to a pub to have a little *sake*, but it's difficult because at 3.30 in the morning we have to visit the master and we can't be smelling of alcohol. And sometimes we go to the whores.'

'Do you have money for it?'

'We get money from home. My mother is always sending parcels, usually there's some special food in them, and sometimes an envelope. That way I got my suit and cap. My father isn't supposed to know, but my mother pities me; she didn't want me to become a monk. And I have an uncle who sends me money every now and then, but he thinks I use it for some Buddhist purpose.'

I couldn't imagine that the head monk didn't know what was going on behind his back. He must have seen the ladder, for he knew every corner of the monastery. And he wasn't only wise, but also very clever.

Sometimes we had a weekend off and I spent them in Kobe, in the house of Leo Marks, but after the visit to the brothel nothing happened there which could offend against the most narrow morality. Leo obviously thought that it wasn't his task to bring me into temptation; he only made sure that I ate well and that nobody troubled me. Sometimes we walked in his garden, or on the beach. Most of all I enjoyed the use of his library. I didn't get up too late, and I meditated in my room.

A holiday came along. I don't remember now why it was a holiday; perhaps it was a national holiday or some day which the Buddhists celebrate. I knew that Leo wasn't in Kobe, and I wondered how I could spend this sudden gift of time. I wandered into the city without any set goal and found a café where jazz records were played on request. I found some trumpet music which I remembered from my days in Capetown and drank whisky. In the afternoon I watched French gangsters killing each other in technicolour. I had another drink and decided to visit Gerald.

'You've been drinking,' Gerald said. 'Have you run away from the monastery? Do I have to take you back?'

He still hadn't forgotten that he had become a disciple of the master before me. When I told him about the official holiday he smiled and asked me to come in.

He lived, as I did, in a Zen temple, with the difference that his temple wasn't a monastery. The priest who took care of the temple seemed to be a simple old man, a friendly quiet priest who had chosen the road of least resistance after his three years in the monastery, a long time ago. He was in charge of the temple and let rooms, while a few old unmarried women kept the temple clean and worked in the kitchen, in exchange for board and lodging.

The central administration of the Zen complex, to which our monastery belonged as well, gave him a small amount every month, enough for repairs and food. The temple was a national monument so the government paid him a little, too. For the rest he had nothing to do, and he did nothing. Once in a while another

Zen priest would visit him. He owned a television set, he read the newspaper, he took part in the temple services of the main temple. According to Gerald he never meditated, because nobody told him to meditate; meditation is only compulsory in the monasteries. Every morning he conducted a short service in the altar room, the old women coming as well and kneeling down respectfully, some twelve feet behind him. He would recite two or three *sutras*, strike his gong, prostrate himself a few times, bow to the altar, and shuffle back to his room. The best rooms in the temple were let to Gerald and he paid, in those days, a sizeable rent, about £10 a month. The priest, who knew that Zen attracts westerners, had prepared the rooms in western style and provided a bed and chairs which had been immediately removed by Gerald who preferred to live Japanese-style. But, and this was a special attraction for me, there was a western-style lavatory, and I would walk the mile and a half between the monastery and Gerald's temple to sit at ease instead of having to perform feats of balance. Gerald invited me to dinner and I helped him, in his small modern kitchen complete with gas stove and refrigerator, cleaning vegetables and cutting meat. He studied my way of working.

'You know,' Gerald said, 'you still haven't learned much. Just look at that. You don't concentrate on what you are doing. You are starting on the next tomato before you have finished the first. You are making a mess of it. You are trying to do two things at the same time.'

I had been getting used to criticism and didn't answer, but after dinner, and after several cups of *sake*, I returned to his remark.

'Zen,' I said, 'as far as I have understood anything about it, is a meditation training, and no more than that. Buddha has found a way which leads to the answer to all questions, and the way is called the eightfold holy path, the noble path. The eight parts are clearly defined, to wit:

1 *right understanding* (understanding the four truths, knowing life is suffering, that the eternal desire, the will to have and

to be is the cause of suffering, that desire can be broken and the breaking of desire is caused by walking the eightfold path)

2 *right intention* (always to intend to walk the path)

3 *right speech* (to be friendly, not to insult or hurt people by words)

4 *right action* (to try to do everything as well as possible)

5 *right means of livelihood* (to earn your living in a decent manner)

6 *right effort* (to continue producing the energy needed to continue)

7 *right awareness* (to know the situation in which one happens to be, so that one can control one's reactions to that situation)

8 *right meditation.*

'That's right, isn't it?'

Gerald moved about on the floor, refilled the *sake* cups and said that I had droned my way nicely through the list.

'I don't like this ticking off, this numbering. But there is no other way to formulate, to define, the path, of course. If you want to mention them all you have to list them one by one. But in reality the sequence isn't right, one moment of the day the second step is important, the next moment it is the seventh, perhaps, I am only giving an example. In fact you need them all, all the time, every moment of the day; one step supports the other and they all belong together, like the weave of a fabric keeps the fabric together.'

'Yes.' I said, and slurred my words, for the *sake* wasn't blending well with the whisky I had been drinking earlier on, even if they were separated by a substantial meal. 'That's what I wanted to say, too. All these steps fit in with each other, but what do we hear in the monastery? Meditation, and meditation again. And the *koan*, but the *koan* is the subject on which one is supposed to meditate. Always the eighth step, never the others, except when you said just now that I wasn't cleaning the tomatoes properly, that would have been the fourth step.'

Gerald began to clear the table and upset a dish which fell and broke.

'Don't say anything, I am not doing this well either. I am getting drunk, or I am drunk already, and then there's something wrong with the second, the fourth, the sixth and the seventh step of my path. And that after many years of training and regular contact with a master. A sad business. But that's the way it is, and there's little I can do about it now. All I can do is be aware of the fact that I am getting drunk, or am drunk already, and try to get through the rest of the evening without accidents.'

'Interesting,' I said, 'a nice example of self-knowledge. But I asked you a question.'

'Meditation,' Gerald said. 'But that's very simple. With a little reflection you'll have the answer yourself.'

The answer annoyed me, it was the sort of answer I kept running into. Even if I asked the address of a dentist the head monk would go to any length of trouble not to give me a clear answer; I would have to find out for myself. As the master said, the answer bubbles up in the disciple's mind, from his own subconscious and the Zen training speeds up a natural process. But how would the address of a dentist bubble up from my own subconscious?

'Tell me something,' I said, 'just try to explain something to me. It will be difficult but you should be able to do it. I don't know why Zen training always harps on meditation, on the *koan*, on the answer to the *koan*. If I knew why it does that I wouldn't ask you.'

'But dear boy, my friend, my fellow disciple,' Gerald said while he refilled my cup again, 'what do you think the answer to a *koan* is?'

'Insight,' I said, 'understanding, wisdom, to know how everything is really connected, the capacity to see through the illusion of existence.'

'Excellent,' Gerald said, 'intelligence can do something. It can't form insight by itself but it can help to come to insight. And now imagine that you have insight, that you have solved a *koan*, an important *koan*, like one of the first *koans* on which you are probably working now. You have given an answer which the master has accepted. You have had *satori*, or a little *satori*, for one *satori* doesn't get you much further than a peep through the crack of the door. Imagine all that—do you think that you can then easily ignore the other seven steps of the path?'

'Ah,' I said, 'so morals sneak in through the back entrance once meditation has opened the way? Somebody who has become enlightened because he has solved his *koan* cannot start a business in drugs, or a war, he can't torture people? Is that what you mean?'

Gerald shook his head. 'Yes, that was what I meant. But now you say so I am not so sure. I know several people who have solved *koans*, they must have had *satori*, and they still do things I can't agree with. They are suspicious, jealous, proud, grabbing, messy, conceited. They are capable of insulting other people just because they feel like doing it. They eat too much and they get drunk. One would think that *satori* would rule out that sort of behaviour.'

'Maybe they would have been worse if they hadn't had *satori*, if they hadn't meditated.'

'Could be,' Gerald said. 'I don't know. Coming to think of it, I don't know anything about *satori* either. And you'll have to go home. It's twelve o'clock. You should have been back by eleven.'

Once outside I noticed that I was very drunk. The walk back to the monastery took me a long time and I had to support myself against endless walls which moved and swayed when I touched them. When I finally found the gate it was closed and the secret latch of the small side entrance was locked as well. I followed the wall till I thought I was near my room and climbed on top of it after having slid off several times.

I saw a patch of green on the other side of the wall and mistook it for part of the vegetable garden. It turned out to be a swamp and I sank in it up to my waist. My clothes were soaked through with slime and mud when I managed to find my room, and I crashed right through my front wall, breaking the lathe work and tearing the paper covering from one end to the other. By that time I no longer cared. I dropped down on my mat, pulled a blanket over me and fell asleep.

The next morning, around eleven, Han-san woke me up. I had missed the morning's meditation, the visit to the master, breakfast and a couple of hours of work.

'What happened to you?' Han-san asked. 'Are you ill?'

I told him what was wrong with me and he hissed between his teeth and disappeared. I thought that he had gone to tell the head monk. This then would be the end of my mystic career, but my head ached too much to worry about it. I took my clothes off, wrapped a towel around my waist and went to have a cold shower in the bathhouse. When I had washed and shaved I found Han-san busy in my room. Within a few hours he had my front wall back to its original state. I helped him as best I could and we had tea together, brought by another young monk. When I went to the head monk to apologise he cut me short.

'Han-san told me,' he said, 'you don't feel well. Are you all right now?'

'A headache,' I said.

'Don't do anything this afternoon then. I'll see you at dinner and if you feel all right you can join the evening meditation.'

I bowed.

That afternoon I stayed in my room and slept till Peter woke me up. He had come in without my noticing, and sat down next to my sleeping bag on the floor, in the lotus position.

'Gerald told me you two had a party last night and that you might be in a bit of trouble. I came to check.'

'Marvellous,' I said, 'I don't think I am cut out for this sort of life. In Kobe I went to the whores and here I get drunk. I wonder if the master and the head monk noticed anything.'

'I suppose they have,' Peter said, 'but it doesn't matter. Nothing is stronger than habit and I don't think that any of us expect a newcomer to break his former habits quickly. You shouldn't exaggerate of course. We had a young American here, some years ago, who used to climb the wall three or four times a week. He even managed to make a girl from the neighbourhood pregnant and a little while afterwards he disappeared for good.'

'And they accepted his behaviour all that time?'

'Yes,' said Peter. 'Even after he left nobody in the monastery

95

said anything against him. There was once a Zen master who said that his first *satori* experience consisted of recognising all people as himself. Everybody he met had his own face.'

He gave me a friendly nod, got up, folded his hands together and bowed. I didn't do anything, I just stared at him. When he left I felt that the atmosphere in my room had thickened, as the master's room would often vibrate with power and tension. Peter had experienced *satori*, I could be quite sure of that. In the monastic hierarchy he was considered to be of the same rank as the head monk. They, together with the master, were beings of a higher order, who wore their bodies as actors wear masks and costumes. Or was I trying to convince myself.

A question to meditate on, I thought, and fell asleep again to wake up when Han-san came to call me for the evening rice.

Twelve

A shameless day and *satori* in the willow quarter

One day a year the Zen authorities declare a general amnesty for all Zen monks. It is a day without rules. The master leaves the grounds and the monks are free. Anything goes. The young monks had often told me about the coming feast and walked about grinning when the day came closer.

'Ha,' Han-san said, 'it'll be marvellous again. Last year we had a lot of fun, but you weren't here then. I would like to see what you are going to do that day. We'll make sure there'll be a good supply of *sake*, and lots to eat. We'll close the gate and we won't let anyone in. If you feel like twisting the head monk's nose, well, twist it. If you want to crash through your front wall again, fine but perhaps you should restrain yourself a little this time because I'll have to do the repairs, of course.'

I told myself to be very careful. I wasn't used to alcohol any more, and whatever the monks intended to do would float on liquor. And what can one do on a day without rules? I should have preferred to retire to my room, with a book and a packet of *shinsei*-cigarettes. To sit in the sun, perhaps, in a quiet corner of the temple garden, or play with the puppies which the monastery's mongrel had produced. They were charming puppies, tiny bundles of fluffy wool who had just learned to walk and performed tumbling games in the graveyard all day long. I knew they were going to be drowned and that there was nothing I could do to prevent their untimely death. What could I, a lay-brother, do with five small dogs? Their barking would disturb the monks during meditation and nobody in the neighbourhood wanted them.

The day came and everyone started it by sleeping late. At about 8 a.m. breakfast started and the monks wandered in and out of the kitchen without clearing the tables—normally the tables were cleared, scrubbed and stacked immediately after meals. I fried some bacon and eggs in the kitchen and made myself a large pot of coffee while the fat cook helped me curiously: bacon and coffee, in his way of thinking, were most exotic. In exchange I helped him to prepare the festive meal, fried noodles, vegetables and sizeable lumps of meat. We were going to have ice-cream as well and I promised to go and fetch it at the last moment as the monastery didn't have a refrigerator. At about eleven the *sake* bottle appeared and the young monks especially got drunk in no time at all. Nobody had any defence against alcohol and as *sake* is drunk quickly, although the cups are quite small, the effect is quickly noticeable. *Sake* is not wine, but a spirit, distilled from rice, and about as strong as whisky or gin.

Han-san sat next to me and dominated the conversation. When the others wanted to say something as well he lost his temper and demanded the right to finish his story. Another young monk, whose face had become as red as a sour plum and whose eyes swam about in blobs of pink jelly, took umbrage and the older monks had to separate the two fighters. Han-san stumped out of the kitchen and I found him, a couple of hours later, fast asleep in the shadow of a gravestone. I sat down near him and made myself comfortable with a thermos flask of coffee and a translation of the famous story of *Shanks' Mare*,* the story of two Japanese good-for-nothings who leave Tokyo because the bill collectors become too active, and wander down to Kyoto along the highway. It's a good description of Japan in the early nineteenth century, and was an appropriate book to read on this day of freedom for the two heroes of the novel solve most of their problems by laughing and running away.

The sun went behind the clouds, it became chilly, and Han-san woke up, cramped on the cold stones.

'Give me some of that coffee,' Han-san said, 'a free day like this isn't much fun really. What can we do with it? I have a head-ache already and the evening hasn't even come yet. The others will probably be milling about in the temple and the head monk

* Ikku Jippensha, *Shank's Mare* (Tuttle, Tokyo, 1960).

is watching them, of course. He hasn't had a drop himself, he is just pretending to join in the fun while he keeps things quiet so that there won't be too much of a mess to clear up to-morrow.'

'What would you like to do?' I asked, 'put on your suit and cap and scale the wall?'

'No,' Han-san said. 'We shouldn't. It's tradition that we amuse ourselves within the walls of the monastery and the head monk will be counting heads all the time. It's a dull life in this monastery. If I had the courage I would become a disciple of Bobo-roshi—he runs a different show altogether.' Roshi means master. I also knew that Bobo is a four-letter word meaning copulation.

'Bobo-roshi?'

Han-san sat up and lit one of my cigarettes, something which he would normally never do without asking; but this time he just grabbed the packet.

'Yes,' he said, 'have you never heard about him? Peter knows him but it isn't like Peter to talk about Bobo-roshi. The head monk knows him quite well, I believe. Bobo-roshi is a Zen master, but different. If you like I'll tell you what I know, but I don't know if it's all true; I only know about him by hearsay and I have only met him once. He seems to be an ordinary man but he laughs a lot and he has a very deep voice and he dresses strangely. He never wears the Zen robes but usually dresses in a simple kimono, like artists do, and sometimes he wears western clothes, jeans and a jersey, like you do. They say he has spent years in a Zen monastery, in the southern part of Kyoto. It's a severe monastery, the rules are applied very strictly, more strictly than here. For instance, I believe they get up at 2 a.m. every day. He is supposed to have been a very diligent monk, rather overdoing things even, making extra rules for himself and all that. But he didn't understand his *koan* and the master was hard on him; whenever he wanted to say something the master would pick up his bell and ring him out of the room. He was treated that way for years on end. He was doing extra meditation, sleeping in the lotus position, trying everything he could think of, but the *koan* remained as mysterious as ever. I don't know how long this situation lasted, six years, ten years maybe, but then he had enough. I don't think he even said goodbye, he just left, in ordinary clothes, with a little money he had saved, or which had been sent to him from home.

Now you must realise that he had been a monk a long time and didn't know anything about civilian life. He had never climbed the wall at night. He was a real monk, sober, quiet, always in command of himself. And there he was, in a sunny street, in a busy city, thousands of people about, all doing something, all going somewhere. He wandered about the city and found himself in the willow quarter, perhaps within an hour of leaving the monastery gate. In the willow quarter there are always women standing in their doors, or pretending to be busy in their gardens. One of the women called him, but he was so innocent that he didn't know what she wanted. He went to her and asked politely what he could do for her. She took him by the hand and led him into her little house. They say she was beautiful; who knows? Some of these women aren't beautiful at all but they are attractive in a way, or they wouldn't have any earnings.

She helped him undress—he must have understood then what was going on. She must have asked him for money and he must have given it to her. Then she took him to her bath, that's the custom here. Your shoulders are massaged and you are dried with a clean towel and they talk to you. Slowly you become very excited and when she feels you are ready she takes you to the bedroom. He must have been quite excited after so many years of abstaining. At the moment he went into her he solved his *koan*. He had an enormous *satori*, one of these very rare *satoris* which are described in our books, not a little understanding which can be deepened later but the lot at once, an explosion which tears you to pieces and you think the world has come to an end, that you can fill the emptiness of the universe in every possible sphere. When he left the woman he was a master. He never took the trouble to have his insight tested by other masters, but kept away from the Zen sect for many years. He wandered through the country and had many different jobs. He was a truckdriver, driving one of these huge long-distance monsters. He also worked as a waiter in a small restaurant, as a dock-worker, and sometimes he joined the beggars and the riffraff of the cities. They say he never forgot the link between his *satori* and sex, and he is supposed to have had many friends and girl-friends. Then he came back and rented a ramshackle house here in Kyoto. He has some disciples there now, odd birds who could never accept the monastic training as we have it here. They do as they please and observe no rules. He works with them in his own way, but he does use the Zen method, *koan* and meditation. The other masters recognise him, acknowledge his complete enlightenment, and never criticise him as far as I know. There are, of course, a lot of young monks who think that life in Bobo-roshi's house is one eternal party; perhaps it is really like that, but I rather think that it isn't.'

I had listened to Han-san with increasing surprise and it took me some time before I could think of an answer.

'So Zen training can be really free?'

Han-san looked at me sadly.

'Free. What is free? Those fellows have to work for their living, that is one discipline to start with. And they meditate, and I am sure it isn't just half an hour when they feel like it. Bobo-roshi may have fetched his *satori* from the whores' quarter but he had been through a long training before he went there. Water suddenly boils, but the kettle must have been on the fire for some time. There's always a preparation. And then he wandered about for many years before he started teaching; that must have been quite a discipline, too. I think that the training in Bobo-roshi's house is just as hard as ours, but it has a different form. You get nothing for nothing, I have learned that. Maybe they have a party there every now and then, but I climb the wall sometimes. And there are many things which our master can teach us.'

Han-san looked very disgruntled and I began to laugh.

'Ha ha. You haven't got the courage to go there, Han-san.'

'You come with me,' Han-san said. 'We have rested and we are sober again and now we can have some cups of *sake*. And when I have drunk enough I'll beat you up.'

And so it happened. Han-san got drunk again and became very troublesome. I think I took him to bed at least four times, and he came back every time and pushed everyone who strayed in his way.

The next day he had a headache.

'Was I very annoying?' he asked when we were working in the vegetable garden together.

'I wouldn't know, Han-san' I said. 'Yesterday we were all invisible. People made out of transparent clear glass. I didn't see you. That's the way it is in Japan, isn't it?'

'That's the way it is,' Han-san said.

Thirteen

Devils are no good, you know that, don't you?

The idea of going into a monastery had been inspired by an English philosophy professor in London, some years before I came to Japan. He had made me read some twenty books, and during a short conversation, when I ran into him accidentally in one of the corridors of the university, I had told him that none of the books he had advised me to read, and none of his lectures had brought me any closer to the truth.

'But what are you looking for?' the professor asked and stood still abruptly, forcing me to stop as well.

'Well,' I said, 'you know. Truth. Why it has all started, and what's the good of it,' and I gestured vaguely about me.

'Absolute truth,' the professor lectured patiently, 'does not emerge from the study of philosophy. Philosophy is a science, and science means approaching truth. By engaging in experiments, by thinking logically, we try to get nearer to truth by determining probabilities. Then we draw conclusions. We say that this is more probable than that, because of this or that reason. But to really know something, to be quite sure of something, no.'

'Then I am on the wrong road,' I said, 'because I want to be quite sure. I want to be absolutely certain that life on earth serves a purpose, because as long as I am not certain I am not content and that's putting it mildly. I sometimes get so depressed, and everything around and in me becomes so utterly hopeless, that there's nothing I can do, except lie down and feel cramps in my stomach.'

'Yes,' the professor said kindly. 'Depression. A well-known phenomenon. Can lead to suicide. Most unpleasant.'

'But how do I get rid of depression? Do you know?'

'Yes,' the professor said and filled his pipe. 'Manual therapy may help and psychoanalysis, of course, but if you ask me, most of it is useless for treating your sort of affliction. What you have is what all mystics have had, and the only way of solving your problem is to join a mystic training. Go to a monastery, find a master, an adept who has finished his training, and he'll cure you or you'll cure yourself.'

He lit his pipe, shook my hand and strolled off, a file bulging with papers clasped under his arm.

The monastery idea of the professor was later combined with what I thought I had learned from books on Buddhism, and the resulting force took me to the master in Kyoto, but the decision involved some time and trouble for the idea of a monastery didn't appeal to me. The word 'monastery' associated itself with 'lifelong sentence.' If I had known that Zen monasteries only keep their monks for three years and that Zen masters will take lay-disciples and don't insist on robes and vows, I would have gone to Japan earlier. When the master accepted me as a disciple the master had made me promise that I would stay for eight months. I had now spent a year in the monastery.

One beautiful summer afternoon, when I was enjoying myself chopping wood near the bathhouse, Han-san came to tell me that the master was waiting for me in his little house. This gave me a fright, for it was the first time the master called me. I saw him every day to 'discuss' the *koan*, and sometimes he said something to me when he met me in the garden, but normal human contact had never been established, except perhaps once when I met him in town. I had been buying some clothes in a department store and on my way back I suddenly saw him in the street, in the middle of a crowd. He wore a simple brown robe like many Buddhist priests wear, and there was nothing spectacular about him. I meant to greet him by performing the formal temple bow (to stand dead still, bow from the waist, allow the hands to glide down below the knees, pause for a few moments at the lowest point, and come back slowly), but he shook his head as if to indicate that the customs of the temple were not applicable to life in the street.

I asked him where he had been, not because I really wanted to know but because that's the way one greets one's fellows in Japan. 'Morning sir, where have you been?' Whoever is addressed like that mumbles something, smiles and goes on. But the master answered my question in full. He explained in detail that he had just been to the dentist and pointed out where the dentist had his rooms. Then he opened his mouth, beckoned me to come closer, and pointed to a bleeding hole in his jaw. It had really hurt, he said. He would have trouble eating for a few days. And the worst was that he would have to go back next week, and probably lose another back tooth. I know everything about toothache and pulling and drilling so I could tell an interesting story as well. Then he wanted to know where I had been and I showed him the jeans and shirts I had just bought. If I hadn't suddenly remembered that he was my teacher I would have invited him to have coffee with me. That meeting had taken place some months ago. Now I was being summoned, by Han-san, the official messenger of the monastery, to go and visit him officially.

I combed my hair, washed my hands, put on a clean shirt, and hurried to his house. On the way I worried. It could be that he wanted to send me down, that my visits to the bathhouse, the weekends in Kobe, my dozing and dreaming in the meditation hall, and my regular simulation of throat-ache to avoid the early morning meditation had finally given him cause to tell me that I might do better by trying somewhere else. In the porch I saw, next to the master's and head monk's sandals, the large shoes which belonged to Peter. Feeling oppressed I knelt down at the door of the master's sitting room and wished my hosts a good afternoon.

'Come in,' the master said, and pointed to where he wanted me to sit. There was no cushion for me. The head monk and Peter didn't have cushions either. A Zen master gives a cushion to a disciple if the latter's training has been completed and although the head monk had finished his *koan* study it didn't mean that he had the master's rank. He still had to show that he could use the insight which he had wrung from his *koan* study. Masters are never in a hurry, and a disciple, provided he is in the later stages of his training, isn't in a hurry either. Everything comes, if you do your best. And if it doesn't come, that's all right too.

'We have called you,' the master said, 'because you have now spent a year with us. You were supposed to stay eight months and we added a few months on to that. You haven't approached us, you have never told us you want to leave, so we may assume that you want to continue your training. We are now going to change your training somewhat.'

He waited a few moments so that Peter could translate. After the misunderstanding which had taken place at the time of Rohatsu he apparently didn't want to take risks.

'In the temple,' the master continued, 'you live among Japanese. We have a way of thinking and living different from what you are used to. Every man has, in essence, the Buddha nature, but the outward appearances differ. The head monk and I understand a little of what goes on inside you, and if we had nothing else to do, we could speed up your training a little. But even if we did have more time we would still be Japanese, and it is possible that you wouldn't understand us because your associations differ. When I am talking about a white crane you may think of a stork, which isn't always the same thing.'

He paused again, and Peter translated while the head monk poured tea. The master held up his cup and we followed his example; we drank formally, elbows up so that the side sleeves of the master's and the head monk's robes hung down in an imposing manner, put the cups down neatly in front of us, and the master continued.

'Up till now the head monk, who is one of my two most advanced disciples (Peter and the head monk smiled but the master gave them an ironic look and said that he used the word 'advanced' because he hadn't been able to think of a more appropriate word), has dealt with you. I want to make a change now. I want Peter to learn what it is like to work with a beginner. Perhaps he may learn something and it won't do you any harm either. That's why I don't want you to stay in the monastery but rather move in with Peter. He will give you board and lodging and tell you what you have to pay him. And you, from your side, will have to behave as if you were his disciple although you'll continue to be mine. I want to see you here every morning and also in the evenings, for meditation. For the rest Peter will have to decide on how you will spend your time and when you will have to meditate.'

He looked at me, and the fierce black eyes stung me, but I didn't look down. I didn't lower my eyes during the daily interviews either, when he asked me what the answer to my *koan* was.

'Think about it and let me know your answer, today or tomorrow.'

'I don't have to think about it,' I said, 'if Peter is agreeable I'll do as you say.'

'That's all right then,' the master said. 'But before you leave I want to tell you a short story. Perhaps you know it. Do you know the story about the gentleman who went to market and bought himself a devil?' I didn't know the story and the master asked us to sit at ease; he lit a cigarette and allowed us to smoke as well. Peter fetched ashtrays and the head monk poured more tea and gave us each a sugar-cake, from an ornamental box which an old lady from the neighbourhood had presented to the master that morning.

Some two hundred years ago a gentleman, who lived by himself in a large house not far away from here, saw a devil in a cage when he was visiting the market: a devil with a tail, yellow skin, and two long sharp fangs—he was about the size of a large dog. The devil sat quietly in a strong bamboo cage and gnawed on a bone. Next to the cage a merchant was watching the crowd and the gentleman asked him if the devil was for sale.

'Of course,' the merchant said. 'Otherwise I wouldn't be here. This is an excellent devil, strong, diligent and able to do anything you want him to do. He knows how to do carpentry, he is a good gardener, he can cook, mend clothes, read you stories, chop wood, and what he doesn't know he can learn. And I don't ask much for him, if you give me 50,000 yen (£50) he is yours.'

The gentleman didn't haggle and paid in cash. He wanted to take the devil home at once.

'One moment,' the merchant said. 'Because you haven't bargained with me I want to tell you something. Look here, he is a devil of course, and devils are no good, you know that, don't you?'

'And you said he was an excellent devil,' the gentleman said indignantly.

'Sure, sure,' the merchant said. 'And that's true as well. He is an excellent devil, but he is no good. He will always remain a devil. You have made a good buy, but only on the condition that you keep him going all the time. Every day you'll have to give him a routine, from this time to that time you have to chop wood, and then you can start preparing the food, and after dinner you can rest for half an hour but then you really have to lie down and relax, and after that you can dig in the garden etc. etc. If he has time to spare, if he doesn't know what to do, then he is dangerous.'

'If that's all,' the gentleman said, and took the devil home. And everything went beautifully. Every morning the gentleman called the devil who would kneel down obediently. The gentleman would dictate a daily programme and the devil would start his chores and work right through the day. If he wasn't working he rested or played, but whatever he did, he was always obeying orders.

Then, after some months, the gentleman met an old friend in the city, and because of the sudden meeting and the thrill of seeing his old buddy again he forgot everything. He took the friend to a café and they started drinking *sake*, one little stone jar after another, and then they had a very good meal and more to drink, and they landed up in the willow quarter. The ladies kept the two friends busy and our gentleman woke up in a strange room, late the next morning. At first he didn't know where he was but gradually it all came back to him and he remembered his devil. His friend had gone and he paid the bill to the women, who looked quite different now from what he remembered the previous evening, and rushed home. When he reached his garden he smelled burning and saw smoke coming from the kitchen. He stormed into his house and saw the devil sitting on the wooden kitchen floor. He had made an open fire and was roasting the neighbour's child on a spit.

The master knew how to tell a story, and the hairs on my head were prickly and hot. Peter told me later that he had heard the story before, but never as gruesomely as this time. When I said goodbye the master put on his friendly old man's face and patted me on the shoulder. Actors, I thought bitterly. Three actors making fun of a bumpkin. Three cats and one mouse. While I am walking in this garden and trying to do my best they sit there and howl with pleasure. Life is a joke. All this trouble to find an answer like that. That devil is no good, but whoever created him isn't any good either. Or do I have to get rid of this idea of creation? The creator created the earth, and with the earth he created the possibility of concentration camps, pain in every possible form, death, suffering, Perhaps there has never been a creator and it is likely that nothing was ever created. And if I have never been created, and therefore do not really exist, it doesn't matter much if I am any good or not. Or not? Shaking my head and mumbling I met Han-san who gave me a worried look and wanted to know what had happened.

'So you will go on coming every day,' he said, and seemed pleased. It seemed that I fulfilled an important part in Han-san's life. He even explained it to me once. He admired me, he said, because I knew how to do many things and I knew such a lot. 'But *what* then?' I asked, because I thought that he could do more and knew more than I. He could sit still for hours on end, repair walls, write Japanese and Chinese characters with a brush, and probably solve *koans* as well.

'Well,' Han-san said and shrugged his shoulders. 'Anybody can do that. And I don't know much about *koans*. But you can drive a car, and you have travelled, and you speak English and German and your own language, and you have books which I can't read and you don't mind who you are dealing with and you entered this monastery voluntarily. If I hadn't been forced to come here the idea would never have entered my head.'

Fourteen

If you don't hold out your hand a Zen master will be murdered

The day I moved, Ko-san, one of the young monks, was expelled from the monastery. If I hadn't met him on his way to a taxi waiting for him at the gate, laboriously lugging a large suitcase and a bundle wrapped in a piece of multi-coloured cotton, the chances are that I would never have noticed his disappearance. Of the monks I only really knew the head monk, the cook, the tall thin Ke-san who often replaced the head monk, and, of course, Han-san, my friend and helpmate. The others I knew by name and face, but I had no contact with them. They lived in another part of the temple and formed, together, a solid block, cemented as a group by their shared activities: the daily begging-trip through the neighbourhood, their work in the gardens, and the cleaning and repairing of the temple. Another reason for not knowing them was that I had been told, by the master and the head monk, not to join them. Three years pass quickly, the head monk said, and it is a hard task to change playful young monks into Zen priests with a sense of responsibility, and give them some idea of what Zen can be. The monks are looking for distraction, and what could be better than a westerner, dumped suddenly into their environment, like a circus-bear who knows tricks?

Han-san was the monastery's messenger, and I could have a certain amount of contact with him, but with the others I could only work; and as soon as a bell or a gong was struck the togetherness came to an end and I had to return to my room, or leave the grounds for a Japanese lesson or the illegal relaxation of a visit to the bathhouse or restaurant, or a walk through the neighbourhood.

Ko-san I knew as a quiet monk who did, mildly and obediently, whatever he was told to do and who had only caught my attention by the lightning speed with which he climbed trees. The fir trees in the garden were cut and pruned regularly and Ko-san, who had special shoes with rubber soles for that purpose, could walk up the trees as if he had been a squirrel in a previous life and had suddenly remembered the fact. I had also noticed that he often missed the meditation periods, for in the hall he sat opposite me and if he wasn't there there was a hole in the monotonous row of black shapes.

I helped Ko-san with his suitcase and asked him where he was going.

He mumbled something about home and stomach-aches, but he looked so sad and despondent that I understood that there was something more serious going on than a simple sick-leave.

Han-san, as always, explained the incident.

'Troubles,' Han-san told me. 'These stomach-cramps aren't so bad; they are more like your throat-ache when you don't feel like getting up in the middle of the night.'

'But I only have to move,' I protested. 'Ko-san is moving out altogether.'

'Yes,' Han-san said. 'He has been sent down, suddenly, this morning. The master and the head monk called him and now he has to go. He can tell his father that he is physically too weak for the monastic life, and now he'll become a farmer I suppose, but perhaps he'll return later.'

Han-san wasn't prepared to clarify the situation further. He was very busy, too, his name was called again, and in the main temple a gong was struck, indicating the beginning of a temple service.

Peter and Gerald told me that it is not exceptional for a monk to be suddenly sent away; it may even be that the monk is trying to do his best but that he is hindered, somehow, by a block within himself, and cannot make any progress. The monastery's authorities will then try, by inflicting a sudden shock and a change of environment, to force a breakthrough. It may be that the monk returns on his own initiative. Perhaps he finds another teacher who is able to get closer to him and with whom he has some special affinity. But it is also possible that the monk will terminate his training, or think that he is giving up his training. 'The *koan* will continue to work in him,' Peter said. 'A *koan* is a time-bomb, a very complicated time-bomb. One day the bomb will explode. It may happen years later, all sorts of winding paths may be walked, anything may have happened, but the master's work is never lost.'

'But when will this bomb explode? In this life? In a next life? And doesn't the monk, or the ex-monk, have to do something himself to cause the flash? Surely it isn't an automatic mechanism which will go off by itself after a certain period of time has passed?'

Peter laughed when I asked the question.

'This life, next life. You have read too much. Haven't you ever considered the possibility that time doesn't exist? That there is nothing but "now"? "Now" you can do something. "Now" is eternity. And if you don't do anything "now" nothing will happen "now".'

It was one of the many answers given to me about which I had the feeling that they were brilliant, deduced from the one and only reality, but which I couldn't make use of because as soon as I started to have a good look at such an answer its message proved to be well outside my reach.

My removal took little time or effort. I had arrived with one suitcase and I left with one suitcase. Peter took the suitcase on his scooter and I caught the tram. He lived at half an hour's walking distance from the monastery, in a four-roomed house with a large garden. I was received in a solemn manner. Peter was waiting for me at the gate. He showed me my room, a large spacious room with the usual niche used by the Japanese to hang a painted or drawn scroll, where they place a vase with a single flower, or perhaps some twigs and dry flowers, beautifully arranged.

He mentioned a very reasonable amount to be paid monthly and took me to his own room where he gave me a cushion (there were no chairs or other European furniture, he lived in pure Japanese surroundings) and poured coffee. I felt as though I was on a formal visit to the head monk and decided to say as little as possible.

'You are here,' Peter said, 'because the master wants it that way. The idea would never have occurred to me. I have always lived by myself and I like living that way. But all right, I'll perform my task as well as I can. Perhaps we can be of use to each other.'

He gave me a questioning look and I nodded. His welcome didn't sound very cheerful, but perhaps cheerfulness is no part of Zen.

'First of all we have to construct a programme for you. I have a pencil and notepaper here. Write down what I am going to tell you—if you don't agree we can discuss it later. Now let me see. At half past three in the morning the master expects us. Then we should have meditated first. It's half an hour's walk, so you'll have to get up at between a quarter past and half past two.'

'Good-day to you,' I thought. In the monastery I got up at 3 a.m. Things weren't getting any better.

'Half an hour's walk takes up too much time,' Peter continued. 'You'll have to have transport, because I am not taking you on my scooter, that's bad for my concentration and for yours as well. A friend of mine owns an old scooter which I can have for nothing, and the garage round the corner will fix it up for you for £20 or £30. You can have a reliable vehicle that way. Once you have your own scooter you can get up half an hour later— we have to be reasonable of course. And you'll be back quicker. Once you are back we'll have breakfast, I'll cook it, and you wash up. Then we'll clean the temple together till you get the hang of it so that you can do it by yourself.'

And so it went on. The whole day was carefully sliced into bits, divided up to the minute. The routine contained at least three hours of meditation, on top of the meditation which I would have to do in the monastery every evening. There was time for work in the garden, time for my Japanese lesson, time to do shopping (that was part of my duties too) and time for naps, twice a day, for half an hour in my room.

After some minor changes we came to a definite daily pro-gramme and Peter asked me to write it all down neatly. When I had showed him the result of my labour he gave me four drawing pins to pin it up inside the door of my cupboard.

'Now pay attention,' Peter said, 'because what I am going to tell you now may amaze you because you are a simple spirit. This programme will come to nothing. We won't have a single day in this house which will follow the routine which we have just created. And logically so, because we have left no space for sudden happenings. It may be that we have visitors, or even that we are busy in the garden and decide to go on, and it may happen that you, because I can't be here all the time to supervise you, will turn the whole programme upside down by sneaking to your room for an extra nap or an hour's secret reading. But when you suddenly wake up again and remember your routine and realise that you are taking part in a training which is supposed to lead somewhere, you can go to your cupboard and all you have to do is look at your watch, and once you know the time, find the right place in your programme, and then do what you should be doing. Follow me?' I followed him. Ten years in Japan had left their stamp on Peter. The Japanese society is stiff with written and unwritten laws, but each law has its clause of escape so that life can still be lived and the number of suicides remains limited.

'All right,' Peter said, 'now have a look at what, according to your programme, you should be doing.'

I went to my room and came back grinning. It was time to take a nap.

'Splendid,' Peter said. 'I am going to have a nap too. When we wake up you can make tea, and after tea we'll work in the garden.'

I spread my sleeping bag on the floor, arranged my Japanese pillow, filled with very small pebbles, but even so a most comfortable support for the head, pushed an ashtray within reach, set the alarm-clock, and lit a cigarette. Peter came in.

'Hey,' he said, 'I won't have that. I don't like smoking much, it's a bad habit and dangerous too. These houses burn easily—they're built of wood, straw and paper, you know.'

'But I always smoke before I go to sleep.'

'And you have never caused a fire?'

'Never.'

'Well, all right then. I suppose I have to try and fit in with your habits as well.'

It was a good beginning. I finished my cigarette, stubbed out the end with care, turned over and fell asleep at once. After half an hour's sleep, so I had learned in the monastery, my resistance to the daily strain would grow considerably. The head monk had even taught me certain exercises so that I would be able to fall asleep quickly, but I didn't need them. All I had to do was close my eyes, grunt, take a deep breath, and I was asleep, and if they tried to wake me up immediately afterwards I felt as if I was being dragged from the end of space. I had to give away three alarm-clocks before I found one which made enough noise to pull me loose, and then only if I placed it on a tin plate and surrounded it with small change.

After the nap I washed my face with cold water, made a pot of Chinese tea and woke Peter who had dug himself into his sleeping-bag and lay, in the shape of an oversize banana, bent between his music-books and a stack of clean laundry.

The energy with which he woke up frightened me. He jumped up, tore the sleeping-bag off his body and swallowed the very hot tea in a few gulps.

'Work to be done,' he said cheerfully, and within a minute we were in his vegetable garden where I had to dig trenches while he brought bucket after bucket, filled with human shit, from the pit under his lavatory, and ladled it with a huge wooden spoon into the trenches. His face was glowing with pleasure and delight as if the brownish-yellow porridge, with bits of toilet-paper sticking from it everywhere, was a delicacy, a special treat for the vegetable garden. I was nauseated and jumped aside every time he passed me, afraid of having the stuff spattered on my clothes.

'Do you think this is dirty?' he asked, very surprised.

'Yes,' I said, 'filthy.'

'Ah, but you have to learn about this. Shit isn't dirty. The entire Japanese economy is based on shit—there are no sewers here, everything is used. One had to do that, with a hundred million people massed on these few islands.'

He pressed a bucket into my hand and told me to fill it up well. When the contents of my first bucket began to slosh about I had to vomit and lean against a fence afterwards. After that the nausea went.

During the first few days in Peter's house it was proved that I could do nothing well. My first attempts at preparing a meal were coupled with black billowing clouds and a nasty burning smell which hung in the kitchen for days. When I cleaned the woodwork with a wet rag the water sloshed down the beams into the straw mats on the floor, which had to be loosened with endless trouble and carried to the garden to dry in the sun. When I wanted to dust the sliding doors (dust collects on the wooden lathe-work which keeps the doors together and is knocked off with a feather-duster) I broke the paper which had been pasted over the thin lathes. When I tried to repair the paper it broke in other places. I struggled through a variety of tasks, spurred on by Peter's sarcasm—he would be so amused at times that he had to turn somersaults and roll about on the floor to give vent to his mirth. He had been brought up on a farm in America and he couldn't imagine that anyone could be as clumsy as I was. The stories he told about me in the monastery must have been very funny, for when I arrived there in the evening for meditation I noticed from the expression on the faces of master and head monk that they had been following my progress and that they enjoyed the daily reports which Peter delivered, breaking them off at some exciting spot so that their interest wouldn't wane.

An old woman who came to clean Peter's kitchen and bath-house every day tried to help me with my work, but if Peter happened to be at home she didn't get a chance. Fortunately he had to work during the day, he taught at a music school, and then, as he had predicted, I would break my routine sometimes to read or sleep, and Tokamura-san, kind old soul, would scrape the pots and repair the other damage. Peter would suddenly rush home, swooping down on us like an eagle from a clear sky, and rage at us both, and I tried to co-operate, realising that what I was trying to do might serve some purpose.

My attempts at meditation met with some success. I was sitting much better now, in a position which looked, if one didn't inspect it too closely, like a half lotus. I had found a spot on Peter's veranda where I felt at home, with a view of the rockgarden. During meditation I didn't look at the rocks and brushwood which complemented each other in artistic patterns, but something seemed to come out of the garden and make my meditation easier. I kept the mosquitoes away by burning a special Japanese incense, a thick green coil giving off a sharp smoke which didn't bother people but frightened off any insect. In the monastery's meditation hall we used a spray-gun, an ideal solution I thought, for I didn't want to have an itch added to my pain, but some of the monks thought the spray-gun a luxury they could do without. Buddha hadn't used insecticides either when he was sitting in the forest in India. They also claimed that it was possible to keep insects away by concentrating in a certain way, but that was a trick which I never learned. The mosquitoes didn't bother me too much, I had got used to their sting, but there was a mean, small black sand-fly, whose bite resulted in swellings which always got infected and even made me run a temperature at times.

What was important to me in those days, and compensated for most of my daily trials, was the scooter which Peter and I had dragged from the back garden of his friend and we pushed to the garage on a wheelbarrow. The rusty, dented structure, carrying the trade-name 'Rabbit', turned out to be a special large size, made for export to western countries, and equipped with a powerful engine with a sound which reminded me of my motorcycle in Cape Town. The garage had promised to return the scooter to its original state and to deliver it to my door within two weeks. I counted the days.

That scooter was a source of joy. Every morning I rode her to the monastery, through a quiet, fast-asleep city in which only policemen, baker's assistants, newspaper boys and late merrymakers were alive. The first time I was stopped by two constables who asked for my papers. I didn't have them on me, but when I told them I was a disciple of the Zen master they both bowed simultaneously and apologised. I met them, or their colleagues, regularly afterwards, and was always greeted by military-style salutes which I would acknowledge by bowing mildly in their direction.

The scooter disturbed the head monk.

'*Koan* study,' he said, 'leads to understanding that all things are connected. All beings are bound to each other by strong invisible threads. Anyone who has realised this truth will be careful, will try to be aware of what he is doing. You aren't.'

'No?' I asked politely.

'No,' the head monk said and looked at me discontentedly. 'I saw you turn a corner the other day and you didn't hold out your hand. Because of your carelessness a truckdriver, who happened to be driving behind you, got into trouble and had to drive his truck on the sidewalk where a lady pushing her pram hit a director of a large trading company. The man, who was in a bad mood already, fired an employee that day who might have stayed on. That employee got drunk that night and killed a young man who could have become a Zen master.'

'Come off it,' I said.

'Perhaps it will be better if you hold out your hand in future when you turn a corner,' the head monk said.

Fifteen

A court lady discourteously treated

Peter, who had lived in Kyoto some ten years and who spoke Japanese fluently, made contact easily with the Japanese. Almost everyone in Kyoto knew him, and it was well known that he was an advanced disciple of the Zen master; apart from that he was fairly famous as a musician who appeared regularly on radio and TV. But it did sometimes happen that he ran into a Japanese who had never heard of him and who would be very surprised when this miracle appeared—a tall, wide-shouldered, blond, blue-eyed westerner who spoke Japanese with a Kyoto accent and understood even the most subtle allusions. If I was present as well the Japanese could relax again, for my knowledge of the language was faulty and my adjustment to the eastern environment only very partial. Occasionally Peter would take me to meet some friend or acquaintance, and we would break the afternoon's routine by making a trip on the scooters. His scooter had the trade-name 'Pigeon', and was light and dainty compared with my roaring 'Rabbit'. I was never allowed to follow him too closely because he claimed to be bothered by the powerful surge of my engine. During a trip through the mountains near Kyoto he held back till I was riding next to him and asked if I would like to visit a hermit. We turned into a narrow mountain-path and arrived after a short ride at a temple on a mountain top, a small Buddhist temple consisting of two buildings surrounded by a high wall and locked in by a solid gate. It was very quiet. Only the wind could be heard, moving the branches of the pinetrees, and a songbird trying out a long pure trill. A panel opened in the gate and I saw the face of a young monk.

'Is he the hermit?'

'No, that is the hermit's servant; he doesn't live by himself.'

The monk, or acolyte, who would have been about sixteen years old, opened the gate, bowed, and bade us welcome. He seemed to know Peter well and showed his metal teeth when he was introduced to me.

'Jan-san,' Peter said, 'another disciple of the Zen master.'

'Welcome, welcome,' the monk said, and brought us to the temple. The sliding doors opened and a man in his early thirties bowed and smiled.

After we had been served tea and cake the hermit told me that he belonged to the Tendai sect and that he had promised to spend seven years in this temple without ever passing through the gate. He was now in his fourth year. It turned out that he spoke English well and Peter didn't have to translate.

'And what are you doing here?' I asked.

'My master gave me a programme!' The Tendai priest said. 'I keep to it all the time. I have a daily routine which starts at 4 a.m. and finishes at 11 p.m. I meditate, I work in the garden, I study English, I chant the *sutras* of our sect, and every day I spend a lot of time on the fire ceremony.'

Later on I had a chance to see the ceremony. Fire forms only a small part of it, for the ceremony consists of a large number of precise gestures and small activities (such as shifting objects about on the altar) which have to be executed with utmost concentration. If the ceremony is done with complete surrender and devotion, the Tendai priest said, peace will result which, in turn, will give rise to insight.

'Do you remember the story of the mirrors?' Peter asked. 'You told me the story once. That story of the Tendai master and the court lady?'

The Tendai priest nodded.

'Would you mind telling it again? My friend has come to Japan to learn something, but so far he hasn't made much progress. Perhaps your story will help.'

The priest laughed.

'I assume that your friend has come to deepen himself. Is that the right word? Deepen?'

Peter said it was.

'Hmm,' the priest said. 'By listening to stories you don't deepen yourself much. You know that surely. Unless, of course, the story comes at exactly the right moment, when the mind happens to be open already. Then perhaps a whiff of insight may arise, and if you are in a certain training, or can produce some discipline, the insight may stay alive and even increase. But I don't mind telling the story again.'

He called the young monk, who brought bowls heaped full of rice and salted vegetables and another pot of green tea, and placed them on small red lacquered tables.

All right then. The story is set in China, when Buddhism had become popular over there and the Zen and Tendai sects were large and strong. Even the emperor was a Buddhist, and a certain court lady felt herself attracted to the mysterious teaching. She visited a number of priests and so-called masters, but didn't find much except splendour and a lot of difficult words. The temples which she saw were beautifully designed and built, she saw magnificent gardens with all sorts of surprise effects and the clergy who controlled this environment pulled holy faces and knew the answer to any question. The lady was intelligent and knew how to observe, and she couldn't rid herself of the feeling that she had been transported into a play, a fascinating show, but a show without substance. She asked and obtained audience with the emperor and described what she had seen.

'Is this Buddhism?' the lady asked.

'Well,' the emperor said, 'the eye wants something too. And religion isn't unhealthy for the people. It gives them something to do and there is always the possibility that they pick up some wisdom from the *sutras* of Buddha. The eightfold path is sublime, and there are priests and monks who try to walk the path, and their example is not without importance.'

'But are there any real masters?' the lady asked.

'Yes,' the emperor said. 'I know a master. He is an

uncouth old man and my predecessors would have cut off
his head if he had addressed them as he addresses me. I have
never been able to get him here, but when I visit him,
and I don't take more than two bodyguards, he may deign
to receive me, if he hasn't got anything better to do.'

'But you are the Son of Heaven!' the lady stuttered.

'Yes, yes,' the emperor said. 'So they say. I myself never
really believed it, and I am quite sure the master doesn't
believe it either. When he speaks to me I am often reminded
of the old Taoist scriptures. You know the sort of thing
I mean, to rule by doing nothing, to speak by remaining
silent, to own the universe by giving up everything.'

'But,' the emperor said, 'if you want to look him up I'll
tell you where he lives. Dress yourself like a common
woman and I will give you two disguised sword-fighters
to defend you on the way. He lives in a deserted part of the
country, a few days' distance from here.'

The court lady was a sincere woman, and courageous,
and she succeeded in finding the temple of the master.
When she arrived a hurricane had passed through the district
and the roof of the temple had been torn off. The master
lived in a ruin.

The master was a man of few words, and unkind words
at that, and he tried to send her away.

'I don't teach. I am an ignorant old man and I live here
by myself. I pass my days in dreams and usually I sit and
stare; what passes through my mind would be of no interest
to you.'

The lady insisted and the master refused again. Finally
she made him a proposition.

'I am rather a rich woman,' she said. 'I should like to
do something for another person, and it wouldn't be very
kind of you to hinder me in this. I should like to have this
temple restored and come back later and spend a week here
to find some peace and be able to listen to you.'

The master listened, thought a little, nodded and shuffled
away. The lady sent workmen, the temple was repaired,

and the lady returned. Instead of a week she stayed three
months. She meditated, she learned the fire ceremony, and
sometimes the master spoke a few words. She did her utmost,
but when it was time to return she had to admit that she
had learned nothing and that the mysteries which she had
tried to comprehend were as veiled as ever. She blamed the
failure on herself and didn't complain, but said goodbye
politely to the master and thanked him for his trouble.

The master was a little upset. His temple had been repaired
beautifully, the lady was a noble and sympathetic woman,
and there she was, rather unhappy and very discontented
with herself.

'Just a moment,' the master said.

The lady climbed down from her horse and bowed.

'Have you got a large room in the palace?'

The lady nodded.

'Good,' the master said, 'see if you can gather together
about fifty mirrors. In about a month I will visit you.
Tell your servants that if they find an old bald-pated bum
at the gate they mustn't beat him up straight away.
Perhaps I shall be able to teach you something after all.'

The lady smiled, bowed again, and rode back to the palace.
When the master came he placed the mirrors in such a way
that they reflected into each other. Then he asked the lady
to sit down in the middle of the room and to look about her
and describe what she saw.

The lady had sat in the lotus position and remained quiet
for a long time.

'I see that everything which happens is reflected in
everything else.'

'Yes,' the master said. 'Anything else?'

'I see that every action of any man has its result in all
other men, and not only in all men, but in all beings, and
in all spheres.'

'Anything else?'

'Everything is connected with everything.'

The master waited but the lady kept quiet.

In the end he grunted.

'It isn't much,' he said, 'but it is something. You haven't come for nothing after all. But there's still much to learn.'

After that he left. He refused all food and drink, and with a nod by way of goodbye walked, bent and a little lame, through her gate, knocking the iron end of his stick against the pebbles of the path.

When she wanted to visit him again later he had died. According to the legend she moved into his temple herself and reached, by doing the exercises which the master had once taught her, the sublime enlightenment.

Peter and I bowed to thank the Tendai priest for his story. He laughed shyly, poured tea and presented cigarettes.

'Yes,' he said, 'it is a good story. My master told it to me. It is a story from our tradition but it could have been a Zen story as well.'

We got up and the priest took us to his gate. He bowed, staying on his side of the threshold, and closed the doors. I looked at the closed gate and was about to kick the starter of my scooter when I saw that Peter was watching me as if he expected me to say something.

'Those mirrors are empty,' I said, 'there is nothing. Nothing reflects, nothing can be reflected.'

Peter walked towards me and gave me one of his rare proofs of friendship; he put his arm around me and pressed me against him.

'The empty mirror,' he said. 'If you could really understand that, there would be nothing left here for you to look for.'

Sixteen

Attempted manslaughter and doing some shopping

It was a winter evening, a long time ago. My father had a fire burning in the grate, and was sitting in his armchair watching the flames. I had brought home two guests for the weekend, friends of my own age, nineteen or twenty years old.

'And what would you like to become?'

'A merchant,' one of my friends said. 'A merchant in the old style. With a business in a seventeenth-century house, and a warehouse with a hoist to be worked by hand so that I could have some exercise. An office with old beams supporting the ceiling. And goods which can be exported so that I could go on a journey every now and then. To smoke cigars and to approach people in a friendly jocular way. To grow a little fat maybe. To be solid. A watch-chain. To have mail, every day, from all parts of the world. To trade in some speciality.'

My father nodded and looked pleased.

'A writer,' my other friend said. 'To travel all over the world, carrying one suitcase and a typewriter. To live on a yacht in the Mediterranean. To publish a book every now and then which produces enough money to finance another trip. And a loft in Amsterdam, and a beautiful woman sometimes.'

My father nodded again but he hesitated and he didn't look very pleased.

'And you?'

Perhaps I said it to annoy him, perhaps I meant it. I said I would like to be a hermit, that I wanted to meditate in seclusion, in a cave or in a small hut in a forest, for months or even years on end. To detach myself from everything, to be free, especially free of myself, of the restless monkey-like jumping about, free of being excited now by this, now by that. And then to find the real peace which should exist somewhere in every man: the great silence.

My father grunted.

'Something ridiculous, of course,' he said. 'Very nice and most extraordinary, but a dream and no more. You'll never be able to do it. You can't be still and by yourself. What you could try is doing something you find on the way. To sit, alone, in a cave, for years on end. Ha!'

Perhaps my father was right.

Not only would I have been a miserable failure as a hermit, and rushed from the cave or the forest to start moving about sadly in the 'world'; here, in the monastery, in spite of the pushing of advanced disciples and the pulling of an everlastingly encouraging master, I couldn't be exactly proud of my progress.

There was, as a daily beginning, the endless fight against laziness. That I had to get up so early hardly mattered. I would have had the same difficulties if I had had to get up at seven instead of three o'clock. Every morning it was the same: my alarm went off, I pressed the button and went back to sleep. Then Peter came in, put me on my feet, sleeping-bag and all, hit me gently in the face, waited till the sleeping-bag had slid down, and then pushed me to the bathroom.

I kept on submitting to this treatment till I began to feel really humiliated and my pride forced me to be clever. I placed the alarm on my chest of drawers, well out of reach, and made myself get up that way. The trick paid off. After that I did sleep late a few times, but I don't think I was to blame then. I was probably too exhausted to wake up and couldn't hear the alarm. But even this success gave little reason for pride. I did get up, and also I meditated regularly, and cleaned the house, but not out of my own free will. I kept to the rules because my environment expected me to keep the rules, because I was being supervised. Voluntarily I did nothing at all, except study Japanese, and I was spending more time on this study than my programme allowed for.

I was, and the discovery pleased me, no exception. Peter had a

Zen monk from another part of Japan to stay at the house. What the monk was supposed to do in Kyoto I don't know, but he came to stay for ten days and he was given a room to himself in the back of the house. He told me that he had joined a monastery because his father and relatives wanted him to, and that he had stayed on after the prescribed three years were over as he wanted to continue his *koan* study. Because of that he had the same status as I could claim: he was a volunteer, a really interested party.

Every morning he stayed in his room till about 10 o'clock. Aha, I thought, he must be meditating. He gets up, just like we do, at 3 a.m. but he is so advanced that he doesn't even bother about a cup of tea and a quick wash; no, he sits down, and meditates for seven hours on end.

Then I heard him snoring one morning. I went to have a look and found him fast asleep. Near his cushions I saw a couple of books, novels by the look of them, and a full astray. So he was reading till the early hours and slept till deep in the morning, exactly what I would do if nobody bothered about me.

'You are not meditating, are you?' I asked him when we were raking the garden together.

'I do in the monastery,' the monk said. 'There I meditate during the prescribed hours and also by myself, in the garden, or in my room, for at least an hour a day.'

I looked at him.

'Yes,' the monk said, 'it isn't as it should be. But that's the way it always is; when I'm not in the monastery I don't practise. I would like to meditate and try to be aware all the time, and try to do everything as well as I possibly can, and be detached and all that, but I forget everything. I read, and I smoke, and I eat, and I sleep a lot.'

'Doesn't your conscience bother you?'

'It does,' said the monk, and got busy again with his rake.

I had wanted to ask him if he had solved his *koan*, but I thought better of it. Anything to do with *koans* is dangerous ground. If he said 'no' it might mean that he *had* solved his *koan*. And if he said 'yes' he might be trying to show off. And whatever he said, it wouldn't bring me any closer to solving *my koan*.

Traditionally Zen monasteries will only admit wandering
Zen monks if they can show proof of having solved a *koan*.

It seems that a monk once knocked on a monastery gate.
The monk who opened the gate didn't say 'Hello' or 'Good
morning', but 'Show me your original face, the face you
had before your father and mother were born.' The monk
who wanted a room for the night smiled, pulled a sandal
off his foot and hit his questioner in the face with it. The
other monk stepped back, bowed respectfully and bade
the visitor welcome. After dinner host and guest started a
conversation, and the host complimented his guest on his
splendid answer.

'Do you yourself know the answer to the *koan* you gave
me?' the guest asked.

'No,' answered the host, 'but I knew that your answer
was right. You didn't hesitate for a moment. It came out
quite spontaneously. It agreed exactly with everything I
have ever heard or read about Zen.'

The guest didn't say anything, and sipped his tea. Suddenly
the host became suspicious. There was something in the
face of his guest which he didn't like.

'You *do* know the answer, don't you?' he asked.

The guest began to laugh and finally rolled over on the
mat with mirth.

'No, reverend brother,' he said, 'but I too have read a lot
and heard a lot about Zen.'

During my last visit to Leo Marks, when I had been wined and
dined again, read another book by van Gulik, and been driven
about in his limousine, he had given me a foot high antique
wooden statue of a Zen master in meditation. I placed the
statue on a special table in my room, burned incense sticks for it,
and used this altar, which I decorated with flowers and fruit, as a
support for my training. The depicted master had a stern expression on his face and sat rigidly in the lotus position, but he did
spread a certain measure of comfort and rest. He symbolised
so I thought, my own attempts, for everything in the monastery

connected with my training had been created by others while this statue had been installed by myself, as proof of the striving of my own soul, even if that soul did not exist.

The statue also helped when, at the end of a long day, I returned to my room. The little master would welcome me with his glass eyes. A little kindness wouldn't be wasted, for Peter seemed to grab any occasion to criticise, and often corrected me when others were present. I made, so he said, too much noise when washing up. I allowed tools to lie about in the garden. I left crumbs on the kitchen floor. I made a mess in the bathroom. I didn't park my 'Rabbit' in the right place. I forgot to close the doors.

I didn't protest, I didn't argue, and I didn't go for his throat. It may have been fear, for he was strong and he had an over-powering personality. But it may also have been because I kept on trying to remember that (a) Peter was only obeying orders, he did what the master had told him to do and I might use this criticism to better my being and thereby empty my being so that I could realise the Buddha nature, and that way achieve *satori*, and (b) nothing is important enough to get upset about.

(b) was more help than (a). With (a) I had some trouble because it went dead against my former way of thinking. As a child and as a boy I had consciously, so far as a child or a boy can be conscious, tried to go against authority. As soon as I had to face criticism I told myself that whoever was supplying criticism had to be wrong, whether he was a parent, a teacher or some other official bearer of truth, and wrong *a priori*. I had come to this conclusion by reasoning that the world in which I found myself was wrong; it was a world filled with injustice and greed, and its inhabitants were murdering, exploiting and torturing each other in many different ways. Anyone who tried to force me to accept this world, whatever method he might be using, could not be right for he was trying to make me accept the unacceptable, and the only way I could save my soul was through anarchy, by trying to destroy the establishment, hoping that something better would grow out of its ruins. Another reason I may have had was that I liked destruction. It seemed more fun than building ugly concrete castles, consisting of money, fame, power and other illusory nonsense which would come to nothing anyway but were grim and forbidding while they lasted. And if I couldn't destroy, I could at least resist.

But now I could no longer resist. I even had to co-operate, as consciously as possible, because this would be the way which would lead me to a point where injustice and greed would be unmasked, as divine or mystic apparitions, useful illusions once I recognise them as illusions.

A moment came when I was busy cutting meat in the kitchen, using a long, very sharp knife. We had a visitor that day, one of Peter's pupils, a Japanese girl who took singing lessons at the school of music where Peter taught. I thought she was a lovely girl and wanted to make an impression. I knew she was coming that day, and I knew who she was, as we had met before. I had prepared myself by putting on a shirt which I thought would look well on me, brushing my hair and shaving carefully, and I had been aware that I had been doing all this to make an impression. Everything had been done consciously: I had been proud of my awareness, aware of my pride, and proud of that awareness again. It went on like this: how clever I am that I know I am so stupid, how stupid I am to think that I am clever, and how clever I am that I am aware of my stupidity, etc.

But while I was busy cutting the meat Peter made a humiliating remark. I can't remember what it was, perhaps he told me to hurry up or pointed out something which I had forgotten. It wasn't so much what he said as the way he said it, for his way of talking was often cutting and derisive. He, the master, I, the slave, the little servant, the tenderfoot supposed to help the experienced wizard—but the tenderfoot couldn't do anything right. Frustrated humiliations surged up in me and erupted in a burst of anger which flashed right through me. I don't believe I raised the arm which held the knife, but I did twist my arm so that the knife pointed his way and there must have been a murderously nasty expression on my face for the girl stepped back and Peter approached me as if he was going close to a vicious dog. He spoke to me, using soft and pleasant words, and my hand relaxed a little so that the knife fell on the floor. When I served lunch I dropped two plates, but Peter said nothing while I gathered up the pieces. I have the impression that his attitude towards me changed from that day, and his method became more positive. Rather than jumping on me when I did something wrong he would praise me when I tried to do something well. Gerald followed this new adventure with interest. He had never been an intimate friend of Peter's but now that I was staying in Peter's house he came to see us regularly. During the weekends he would meditate next to me on the veranda and Peter sometimes joined us. We would sit 'formally', and even use a temple bell which we rang at twenty-five minute intervals.

'You're raving mad,' Gerald said, one afternoon when he had dropped in unexpectedly and we were having coffee together in the moss garden. 'Why do you submit to this guy? Do you think it will get you anywhere?'

'I think so,' I said. 'It's part of the training, and since the master thought of this arrangement, I can assume that the master knows what he's doing.'

'Hmmm,' Gerald said. 'I wouldn't be able to do it. I should leave. I can put up with self-discipline, but they mustn't push me around. But perhaps you need this type of treatment, maybe you'll get self-discipline this way—for one thing is certain, you haven't got it. If they put you in a house by yourself you would just mess about.'

'Thank you kindly,' I said, 'Peter is friendlier than you are.'

'Nonsense,' said Gerald and gave me a cigarette. 'I am your friend, he is your boss. If a friend makes an unpleasant remark it's all right.'

I began to realise that I should never be able to solve the *koan*, although I was quite convinced that the *koan* did have an answer. My visits to the master had degenerated into a dumb silence on my side. I had given all the answers I could think of, so what else could I do? I went because the visits were part of the daily routine, because I enjoyed riding through the silent city, because I admired the master, and out of irritation. He knew the answer, I did *not* know the answer. Every morning I saw a man who knew all the answers, sitting on a little platform, an old man with slanting eyes and pouring out strength.

My lack of a result didn't depress me. I was far too busy digesting the new impressions of my life with Peter, with the many different tasks of which my life consisted, and which in themselves were all exercises. Best of all I liked the daily shopping. Before the scooter arrived I would walk, every morning, through a narrow street formed by many stalls, jostling each other for space. I bought vegetables, meat, tea and all sorts of Japanese specialities which formed, because they were cheap, part of our daily menu. I carried a basket on my arm but I only felt ridiculous the first day. The shopkeepers didn't laugh, and the general friendliness which I encountered everywhere put me at ease. When I had the scooter I would ride her slowly through the street and the stall-holders would put my purchases, very carefully, in the basket which I had tied behind me. Everyone knew what and how much I needed, and kept small change ready so that I could pay quickly. The quiet rhythm of this daily trip fascinated me and every day I tried to perfect the many small activities which were part of this practice. I think it was one of the very few at which I became more or less an adept.

But while I amused myself with novelties, Gerald had reached a dip in the path, and seemed very depressed. His eyes were dull, he began to walk in a slouching manner and his conversations were toneless and negative. To cheer him up I told him a story which I had heard Peter tell some time ago, when I was still living in the monastery.

Once a Zen monk drew attention to himself by his supreme diligence. He got up earlier than the other monks, spent more time on meditation, sang the *sutras* with concentrated awareness, excelled at playing the temple drum, never lost his temper and tried to do everything as well as possible. He behaved like this for a number of years and was made head monk. One morning, when he was walking in the temple garden, he admitted to himself that he had spent sixteen years in the monastery and that he hadn't solved his *koan*, his first *koan*, the *Mu-koan*. The other monks, and most of them had spent only three years in the monastery, had not only solved the *Mu-koan* but many other *koans* as well. He was the only one who had never shown any progress, real progress, for all his other achievements didn't count.

He had, of course, thought of this before, but he had never allowed himself to become depressed. Buddhism, when practised well, creates two feelings, two pillars on which the Buddhist life is built. It creates compassion, and it creates detachment. To be detached is to be free. To be free leads to equanimity. But now, after sixteen years of continuous trying, the whole thing became too much for him. 'A moment will come,' the monk reflected, 'when one has to admit failure. My monastic training has led to nothing. I have wasted sixteen years. And if this is true, I am leaving.'

He went to the master's room and, without asking for permission to enter, strolled up to where the master was sitting and said 'Master, I am off'. The master looked at him. He didn't seem surprised or disappointed. He nodded and said that the monk should do as he thought best. The monk gathered his few belongings and left the monastery. He found a deserted temple in the mountains, moved in, and and gave up all further attempts to solve his *koan*. He got up up at six in the morning, worked in the garden, repaired part of the roof so that it stopped leaking and fixed the sagging floor, and twice a week he went to the nearest village to beg for a little rice and money. He didn't give up Buddhism, for he still believed that Buddha had successfully finished the eightfold path, but he was sure that he, the monk, would never go that far and so he stopped caring. He intended to live the rest of his life in complete indifference, without being irritated by master or *koan*.

After a few months the monk was sweeping the courtyard of his temple and his broom struck a pebble which shot against the bamboo fence, making a sharp sound. This unexpected sound broke something in the being of the monk and suddenly he knew the answer to his *koan*. He dropped the broom, ran all the way to the city, and arrived panting at the monastery gate where found the master waiting for him.

'Yes,' Gerald said, 'and not only had he solved his first *koan* but he knew all answers to all *koans* and he lived long and happily. He became a Zen master and he had many disciples. But I also know a story, about another monk, not so long ago. This monk was given a modern version of an ancient *koan*. The ancient *koan* is "Stop a wild horse which is charging straight at you"; the modern version says "stop the Inter-city train coming from Tokyo". Do you know what this monk did?' Gerald asked. 'I'll tell you what this monk did. He meditated for years and years on this train, and one day he walked to the tracks and threw himself at the Inter-city coming from Tokyo. And in one split second there was nothing left of him and he was quite dead.'

I must have looked startled, and got up to go to my room.

'Wait,' Gerald said, 'I know another real-life story. In Tokyo there are some Zen monasteries as well. In one of these monasteries, quite recently you know, last year, or the year before, there was a Zen monk who happened to be very conceited. He refused to listen to whatever the master was trying to tell him and used the early-morning interviews with the master to air all his pet theories. The masters have a special stick for this type of pupil. Our master has one, too, you will have seen it, a short thick stick. One morning the master hit the monk so hard that the monk didn't get up any more. He couldn't, because he was dead.'

'Isn't that against the law?' I asked.

'Law, what law?' Gerald said. 'The head monk reported the incident to the police, but the master was never charged. Even the police know that there is an extraordinary relationship beween master and pupil, a relationship outside the law.'

When Gerald started his motorcycle and rode slowly through the gate I understood that I hadn't cheered him up.

Seventeen

Is a cloud a member of the sky?

I had now spent a year and a half in Japan. Leo Marks was introducing me to his acquaintances as 'my Buddhist friend'. But I had never become a Buddhist. When I paid my monthly 2000 yen (£ 2) to the head monk I told him that I would like to become a Buddhist, to enter the religion officially.

The head monk put the money into his drawer, drew some artistic characters in his ledger and noted on a strip of paper: 'Jansan, 2000 yen', and the date. The strip of paper was glued to the wall of the corridor, where it became the last miniature paper flag at the end of a row of thousands of strips. When the corridor was full he would tear them all down and begin again.

'Well,' he said, 'it can be done, of course. But it's up to the master really. He is the high priest and he decides about an important matter like this. I'll mention your request and you'll hear from us.'

About a week later Han-san came to tell me that the master was expecting me. The master was having dinner when I came and I waited, kneeling on the floormat, till he had finished. He never had his meals with us but was served, three times a day, a tray with covered bowls: a bowl of rice, a bowl of vegetables and a bowl of soup; and a pot of green tea. The distance from the kitchen to the master's little house was about a quarter of a mile and his food, especially during winter, must have been cold many times. I pitied him; it would have been better if he had shared our meals. We could always have second helpings by folding our hands and staring at the cook while he was serving—we weren't allowed to point but we could indicate the required dish by looking at it and shaking our heads if he got it wrong. The master had to satisfy himself with whatever was brought to him.

While I waited I tried to imagine how this man lived. Every morning he had to get up at three o'clock, then he saw twenty or more disciples, each at a different stage of development, each in his own world, most of them working on different *koans* from different angles, with all sorts of blocks and problems and wrong or half-baked ideas. Then, after that, perhaps a nap. Then breakfast, work in the garden, or his job in the main temple. He was the high priest of a large complex of Zen temples and had to supervise them all. He had to know what the Zen priests in the neighbourhood were doing and guide them when necessary. One of the temples near us was a home for the elderly and two young priests were in charge, looking after the old men and women. There had been a scandal when one of the priests had gambled and lost a large part of the temple's funds. The master had taken care of the crisis and the young priest had been sent on a pilgrimage. The master had spent a lot of time on the priest, trying to find a way of using the incident for the priest's benefit. Perhaps he had given him a fresh *koan*, or he may have insisted that the priest solved the last *koan* he was working on, when he finished his three years in the monastery.

The master also went off on lecturing trips now and then, visiting the large cities, speaking to whoever showed interest in Zen, travelling during the months when our discipline was relaxed. And when he returned from such a trip he would have to deal with us again. I knew he had two ways of relaxing: he would watch baseball on TV and when an important match was on he would lock his house and nobody could see him. He would also go to the cinema sometimes, but only when he could see a picture connected in some way with Africa; he liked animals and the jungle-lush, tropical vegetation. I had even witnessed a difference of opinion between master and head monk. The master wanted to go to the cinema and asked the head monk for money. The master never had any money, because the monastery's funds were in the hands of the head monk. The head monk refused.

'You have been ill. You are supposed to stay in and sleep in the afternoons. You have a weak heart.'

'Maybe,' the master said, 'but I want to go to the cinema *now*. It's the last day this picture is on, I looked it up in the newspaper. Who knows if and when the picture will come again. There's an elephant-hunt in it and I must see it.'

In the end the monk gave in, on condition that the master took a taxi and Han-san went with him in case he became unwell.

Our master, in fact, was a pleasant man of simple habits. I knew that some high priests of the sect enjoyed heading processions, marching along in gold-coloured robes, protected by huge sunshades carried by acolytes. They insisted on being addressed by their proper titles and if you had had tea with them you had to leave the room walking backwards. But one of these high priests, who was also a Zen master, had shocked his public by joining a procession dressed in a cheap house-robe, and wearing plastic bath-sandals. Later he had left his palatial temple and gone to India, as a deck passenger, to visit the holy places. He begged on the way, for he had taken no money, begged with his bowl, as the rule prescribes. He took only an extra kimono, some underwear and his toilet gear, a staff and his bowl. He was away for two years. The priests were annoyed when he came back. They had expected him to travel in style; he was, after all, a high priest, comparable to a bishop or a cardinal. He could have travelled first class and taken monks with him, as servants. The Buddhist church is no longer rich—in 1946 most its posessions were taken away—but there's still some money.

The master had finished his meal and looked at me.

'I hear you want to become a Buddhist.'

'Yes,' I said. 'I have been your disciple for some time now, but I have never entered the faith, or the church, or whatever I should call it. I should like to do so now.'

'It can be done,' the master said. 'We have a special ceremony for this purpose. Quite an impressive ceremony really. All our monks, and also all priests connected with the monastery in one way or another, will come. They will all dress in their best robes. I'll wear the garb which you'll have seen me in before, at New Year for instance; the robe is uncomfortable because brocade is heavy, but it looks well. *Sutras* will be chanted and you'll have to come forward and kneel down and I'll ask you some questions to which you'll have to answer 'yes'. You'll have to declare that you are seeking your refuge in Buddha, in the Teaching, and in the Brotherhood of Buddhists. You'll also have to confirm that you will refuse to enter Nirvana till all living beings are ready to become part of the ultimate reality.

Then I'll wave my horsehair brush and the *sutra* chanting will begin again and Gi-san will play his drum and the head monk and Ke-san will strike their gong and after that there will be a feast for monks and guests. It can be organised. I'll have to ask the head monk to find a suitable date for the ceremony.'

He looked at me. I didn't know what to say. It seemed a very acceptable proposition. But it seemed that the master was expecting something.

'All right then,' I said in the end. 'Many thanks for your trouble.'

He nodded. I thought the interview had ended, bowed and got up. When I was near the door the master called me back.

'There's something I wanted to ask. Why do you want this ceremony to take place? Do you think it will do something for you?'

I had to admit that I didn't think so.

'Do you think that, by becoming a Buddhist, you'll get closer to solving your *koan*?'

No, I didn't think so.

'Hmm,' the master said and turned away. The interview was now really at an end and I left the room.

In the garden I looked for Han-san and found him loading cucumbers into a wheelbarrow.

'Are you a Buddhist?' I asked.

Han-san might be a simple country-lad but he was quick on the uptake.

'I?' he asked innocently. 'I study Zen Buddhism'; (literally translated he said 'I do Zen Buddhism study').

'Yes,' I said impatiently, 'I know. But are you a Buddhist?'

'You know,' Han-san said, 'that "I" don't exist. I change all the time. Every moment I am different. I exist in the way a cloud exists. A cloud is a Buddhist, too. You call me "Han-san" and pretend that I was yesterday what I shall be to-day. But that's your business. In reality there is no Han-san. And how can an unreal Han-san be a Buddhist?'

'Don't be so intricate' I said. 'All I ask you is whether or not you are a member of the Buddhist brotherhood.'

'Is a cloud a member of the sky?' Han-san asked.

I gave up. The ceremony was never mentioned again.

Eighteen

Whatever ends begins

'God is good' the curate said. It was Sunday afternoon and I was staying in Leo Mark's house. The sun was shining in the library and I had opened the windows so that I could hear the sea. The curate was also staying with Leo; Leo's house was a free hotel for wandering bums.

'As long as they shave,' Leo said, 'and close their mouths while they are eating.'

I had met sea captains in his house, who had taken old ships to Japan as scrap for the blast-furnaces. And writers. Travelling businessmen. And now the curate.

'Why is God good?' I asked.

'Because the canary is singing so beautifully.'

Near the open window Leo's canary was whistling away, a jubilant song, full of complicated trills and clear prolonged notes.

'Very true,' said Leo, who had come in without us noticing him, 'God is good'.

Two Buddhists and a curate in complete agreement.

A few days later I was riding my scooter along a precipice. Peter had left the city for a day and I had broken my programme to go out on a trip. Kyoto is surrounded by mountains and I had ridden off without looking at the map. After half an hour I saw no more people. I was riding on a mountain path meant for mountaineers. I saw bits of forest, alpine meadows, and sometimes a glint of Lake Biwa, far below me. Near the precipice I thought that I could, by twisting the handlebars a little, solve a lot of problems very easily. A crumpled scooter and a broken body, and the world, the universe, would cease to exist.

I parked the scooter and sat on an overhanging piece of rock, dangling my legs into the empty sky. The merest self-inflicted push and whoops, China gone and the 700 million Chinese too.

But how about my soul? Buddha had always refused to answer the question. Soul or no soul, life after death or no life after death, an empty question. Walk the eightfold path and the question will drop away by itself, later, now, it doesn't matter. But I was sitting on a rock with my legs stuck into nothing. If I entered Nothing altogether, what would be left over? And suppose something were left, where would it go? Heaven or Hell? The hell of the suicides, a sad sphere filled with sad shuffling shapes, complaining transparent shadows? I pulled in my legs, walked back to the scooter and was back within an hour. On the way I hardly looked at the landscape and the busy farmers and their women folk, working in their picturesque kimonos. I tried to come to the end of my line of thought. What had I learned, after a year and a half of falling over and getting up? That I had to do my best, that I had to try and do everything as well as possible. But I could have learned that in Rotterdam. Dutchmen, and the inhabitants of Rotterdam in particular, do their best; it's a national custom. All I would have to do is imitate my environment, which should be the easiest exercise in the world; it is much easier to join one's examples than to go against them.

But they managed to teach me something else here. Not only has one to do one's best, one must, while doing one's best, remain detached from whatever one is trying to achieve.

Ke-san the thin assistant to the head monk had told me, while I was helping him in the kitchen, the story of the Zen priest and the moss-garden.

A priest was in charge of a small Zen temple, an island of silence and beauty, a few miles out of Kyoto. The temple was famous because of its garden and the priest had been given the temple because he liked nothing better than gardens and gardening. Next to his temple there was another, smaller temple. A very old Zen master lived there, so old that he couldn't have disciples any more. The priest looked after

the old master but there was no official master/disciple
relationship. The priest had given up his *koan* study years ago.

The priest was going to have guests, and he had been
busy all morning perfecting his garden. He had raked all the
fallen leaves together, and thrown them away. He had
sprinkled water on the moss, he had even combed the moss
here and there, he had put down some leaves again, in the
right places; and when finally, he stood on his veranda and
contemplated his garden, could only tell himself that his garden
was, in every respect, as it should be. The old Zen master
had been watching the priest's work with interest while he
leant on the fence which separated the two temples.

'Isn't it beautiful?' the priest asked the master. 'Don't you
think that the garden is now as it should be? My guests will
be coming in a little while and I want them to find the garden
as the monks who originally designed it meant it to be.'

The master nodded. 'Yes,' he said, 'Your garden is
beautiful; but there is something missing, and if you'll
lift me over the fence and put me down in the garden for a
moment I'll put it right for you.'

The priest hesitated, for he had got to know the master
a little and he knew that the old man could have extraordinary ideas. He couldn't refuse of course. A master's will is
law, and that his master happened to be retired didn't
change the rule.

When he had lowered the master carefully into his garden
the old gentleman walked slowly to a tree, growing
in the centre of a harmonious rock and moss combination.
It was autumn and the leaves were dying. All the master
had to do was shake the tree a little and the garden was
full of leaves again, spread out in haphazard patterns.
'That's what it needed,' the master said. 'You can put me
back again.'

According to Ke-san the priest had broken down and wept
and stamped his feet and that wasn't, said Ke-san, what he should
have done. Right, I thought, after my trip along the precipice.

So that's what matters. To do your best and be detached. To come to the point where everything you have been trying to do comes to nothing, and be unmoved. Equanimity. That's all I have been able to learn. A little theory. It has taken me a year and a half. I doubt whether I can practise the theory.

I spent the rest of the day doing nothing in particular. There would be no meditation in the monastery that evening, and I had nothing to do. I could have meditated in my room, studied Japanese or worked in the garden. I could have followed the daily routine, but I didn't feel like it. Peter came home that evening and I asked him if he would mind telling the head monk that I wanted to have three days off. The master was ill, so I wouldn't miss any of the early-morning visits.

'Why?' asked Peter.

I told him that I wanted to lock myself in my room for three days and meditate continuously.

'You can't do it' Peter said.

'I know I can't do it' I said. 'I'll have to spend some time sleeping and eating, but I can try, can't I? To try it won't hurt me.'

Peter didn't like my plan. He tried to talk me out of it, but I insisted. I was convinced that I should do something spectacular, that I should break my daily rhythm, that I had to get out of my depression some way or other, and this seemed the best solution.

'Wait till the master is better, and talk to him about it,' Peter said.

I didn't want to wait. It was now or never. In the end he gave in.

I would start the next morning, at 3 o'clock, and stay in my room for three times twenty-four hours on end. If I had to go to the lavatory, or to the kitchen, he would pretend I wasn't there.

The exercise came to nothing. After half a day I left my room. I couldn't sit still, the room was too small, the walls moved in and suffocated me.

Peter tried to comfort me but I was now so depressed that nothing he said made any impression. The whole Buddhist adventure now seemed one huge failure, and I wanted to leave.

There was no longer any reason to stay in Japan. I didn't know what I wanted to do. There was enough money left for a boat-trip to Europe and some six months' modest living. I assumed that I would be able to find a job within that half year, a simple manual job if need be. I could find a room in Paris or Amsterdam and continue my meditation during the evenings.

Peter, to my surprise, lost his temper. Perhaps he was worried about what the master would say to him, or perhaps he felt personally insulted by my failure—perhaps he thought that my failure was partly his failure. I didn t listen to Peter, but walked to the gate without saying anything and started my scooter. That same evening I rode to Kobe and took a room in the harbour quarter. The next day I booked a passage to Marseilles on an old French steamer, third class. They wouldn't give me fourth class. Fourth class is steerage, and the shipping clerk said that the steerage passengers would pass the time drinking, fighting and gambling and he didn't want a dead white man on the company's conscience.

The boat would leave in a month's time. A few days later one of Leo's acquaintances met me in the street and told me that Peter had telephoned Leo and that they were now both looking for me. I didn't want them to waste their time and called Leo from the nearest telephone booth, telling him that I was safe and on my way to Europe. He asked me where I was staying and when I came back to the hotel I found his car waiting for me. When Leo saw me he shook his head but didn't comment. He took me to his house and Peter came that evening to try and talk me into coming back. I refused. He offered to find me a job so that I could stay in Japan for a number of years. I could work for one of the film studios in Kyoto as a bit-player, or he might even get me a proper job as a correspondent and public relations man in a mercantile company. When I kept on refusing he became angry again and left, mumbling a farewell. Leo, on the contrary, showed no emotion whatever. I wanted to go back to my hotel. I didn't want to live at Leo's expense for a month.

'You can pay me,' Leo said, and worked out how much the hotel would have cost me. The money I gave him was passed on to the servants who all refused to take the tips I offered them when I left.

Three days before the ship sailed I rode to Kyoto to say good-bye to the master. The head monk gave me tea, didn't show any disappointment, and took me to the master's house. The master received me in his living room. He gave me a cigarette and sent the head monk to the meditation hall to fetch a stick, the sort of stick which the monks used to hit each other. He drew some characters on it with his brush, blew on the ink, waved the stick about, and gave it to me.

'The characters mean something which is of importance to you. I wrote down an old Chinese proverb, a saying taken from the Zen tradition. "A sword which is well forged never loses its golden colour." You don't know it, or you think you don't know it, but you have been forged in this monastery. The forging of swords isn't limited to monasteries. This whole planet is a forge. By leaving here nothing is broken. Your training continues. The world is a school where the sleeping are woken up. You are now a little awake, so awake that you can never fall asleep again.'

The head monk looked at me kindly and the master smiled. The heavy gloomy feeling which hadn't left me in Kobe fell away from me. I bowed and left the house.

When the ship detached itself from the quay Leo Marks and Han-san stood next to each other on the wharf. A very tall wes-terner and a very small easterner. Leo waved and Han-san bowed. Then they disappeared in Leo's limousine.

I went into the bar and ordered a cold beer.